Daphne du Maurier was born in London and was educated at home and in Paris. Her first novel, *The Loving Spirit*, was published in 1931, since when she has written many highly successful novels, including *Rebecca, Frenchman's Creek* and *Jamaica Inn*. Disliking town life, she lives in Cornwall.

Also by Daphne du Maurier
in Pan Books

fiction

Rule Britannia
The King's General
The Progress of Julius
I'll Never Be Young Again
Rebecca
Jamaica Inn
Frenchman's Creek
The Scapegoat
Mary Anne
The Loving Spirit
The Birds
My Cousin Rachel
The House on the Strand
Castle Dor
The Rendezvous

non-fiction

Golden Lads: Anthony Bacon, Francis and their Friends
The Winding Stair: Francis Bacon, His Rise and Fall
Myself When Young (autobiography)

DAPHNE DU MAURIER

THE
REBECCA NOTEBOOK
and other memories

Pan Books
London and Sydney

"Someday I'll Find You", permission granted,
Chappell Music Publishers, London

Permission granted to quote from Miss Frith's book,
Leaves from a Life

"Charmaine" reproduced by permission of Keith Prowse
Music Publishing Co. Ltd., 138-140 Charing Cross Road,
London WC2

Lines from *The Uncelestial City* by Humbert Wolfe,
reproduced by kind permission of Ann Wolfe

First published 1981 by Victor Gollancz Ltd
This edition published 1982 by Pan Books Ltd,
Cavaye Place, London SW10 9PG
© Daphne du Maurier
ISBN 0 330 26826 0
Printed and bound in Great Britain by Collins, Glasgow

CONTENTS

THE REBECCA NOTEBOOK
AND EPILOGUE

INTRODUCTION

It is now over forty years since my novel *Rebecca* was first published. Although I had then written four previous novels, *The Loving Spirit, I'll Never Be Young Again, The Progress of Julius* and *Jamaica Inn*, as well as two biographies, *Gerald: A Portrait* and *The du Mauriers*, the story of Rebecca became an instant favourite with readers in the United Kingdom, North America and Europe. Why, I have never understood! It is true that as I wrote it I immersed myself in the characters, especially in the narrator, but then this has happened throughout my writing career; I lose myself in the plot as it unfolds, and only when the book is finished do I lay it aside, I may add, finally and forever.

This has been more difficult with *Rebecca*, because I continue to receive letters from all over the world asking me what I based the story on, and the characters, and why did I never give the heroine a Christian name? The answer to the last question is simple: I could not think of one, and it became a challenge in technique, the easier because I was writing in the first person.

I was thirty years old when I began the story, jotting down the intended chapters in a notebook, and I am now in my seventy-fourth year, with memory becoming hazier all the time. I apologise for this, but it cannot be helped. All I can tell the reader is that in the fall of 1937 my soldier husband, Boy Browning, was commanding officer of the Second Battalion, Grenadier Guards, which was stationed in Alexandria, and I was with him. We had left our two small daughters, the youngest still a baby, back in England in the care of their nanny, with two grandmothers keeping a watchful eye.

Boy—Tommy to me—and I were living in a rented house, not far from the beach, Ramleh I believe it was called, and while he was occupied with military matters I was homesick for Cornwall. I think I put a brave face on the situation and went to the various cocktail parties which we were obliged to attend, but all I really wanted to do was to write, and to write a novel set in my beloved Cornwall. This novel would not be a tale of smugglers and wreckers of the nineteenth century, like *Jamaica Inn*, but would be set in the present day, say the mid-twenties, and it would be about a young wife and her slightly older husband, living in a beautiful house that had been in his family for generations. There were many such houses in Cornwall; my friend Foy Quiller-Couch, daughter of the famous "Q," with whom I first visited Jamaica Inn, had taken me to some of them. Houses with extensive grounds, with woods, near to the sea, with family portraits on the walls, like the house Milton in Northamptonshire, where I had stayed as a child during the First World War, and yet not like, because my Cornish house would be empty, neglected, its owner absent, more like—yes, very like—the Menabilly near Fowey, not so large as Milton, where I had so often trespassed. And surely the Quiller-Couches had told me that the owner had been married first to a very beautiful wife, whom he had divorced, and had married again a much younger woman?

I wondered if she had been jealous of the first wife, as I would have been jealous if my Tommy had been married before he married me. He had been engaged once, that I knew, and the engagement had been broken off—perhaps she would have been better at dinners and cocktail parties than I could ever be.

Seeds began to drop. A beautiful home . . . a first wife

... jealousy ... a wreck, perhaps at sea, near to the house, as there had been at Pridmouth once near Menabilly. But something terrible would have to happen, I did not know what ... I paced up and down the living room in Alexandria, notebook in hand, nibbling first my nails and then my pencil.

The couple would be living abroad, after some tragedy, there would be an epilogue—but on second thoughts that would have to come at the beginning—then Chapters One, and Two, and Three ... If only we did not have to go out to dinner that night, I wanted to think ...

And so it started, drafts in my notebook, and the first few chapters. Then the whole thing was put aside, until our return to England in only a few months' time.

Back home, Tommy and his battalion were stationed at Aldershot, and we were lucky enough to rent Greyfriars, near Fleet, the home of the great friend in the Coldstream Guards who had taken over from Tommy in Alexandria. Reunited with the children, and happy in the charming Tudor house, I was able to settle once more to my novel *Rebecca*. This much I can still remember: sitting on the window seat of the living room, typewriter propped up on the table before me, but I am uncertain how long it took me to finish the book, possibly three or four months. I had changed some of the names too. The husband was no longer Henry but Max—perhaps I thought Henry sounded dull. The sister and the cousin, they were different too. The narrator remained nameless, but the housekeeper, Mrs. Danvers, had become more sinister. Why, I have no idea. The original epilogue somehow merged into the first chapter, and the ending was entirely changed.

So there it was. A finished novel. Title, *Rebecca*. I wondered if my publisher, Victor Gollancz, would think it stupid, overdone. Luckily for the author, he did not. Nor did the readers when it was published.

Its success was such that a year later I adapted the story

for the stage, then later the film rights were sold. War came in 1939. We moved from Greyfriars to Hythe, to the Senior Officers' School where Tommy became commandant. I forgot all about *Rebecca*, if its readers had not. And it may have been because of its popularity that I was asked, some eight years later, to contribute an article to a book entitled *Countryside Character*. I called my article "The House of Secrets," and this can be read in the present volume.

And what became of the original notebook? That is another matter, which I will tell briefly.

The Hitchcock film of *Rebecca* became an even greater success than the book, and was made—I think I am correct in this—around 1940, in the States. Then, some years later, a suit for plagiarism was brought against Selznick International Pictures by the family of a Mrs. MacDonald —I trust I have the name right—who said the story was a copy of a novel she had written called *Blind Windows*. I had never heard of Mrs. MacDonald or her *Blind Windows*. The novel was sent to me, and I glanced through it. It was nothing like my *Rebecca*, save for the fact that the man in the book had been married twice. Nevertheless the suit was brought, and I was called as a witness for the defence.

So in 1947 I went to America with Nanny and my two younger children—I had a boy of six and a half by then, and Tessa, the eldest daughter, was at boarding school— and once in New York I stayed with my American publishers, Nelson and Ellen Doubleday. They became the dearest of friends. My only memory of the plagiarism suit was that the notebook was produced in court, and after cross-questioning the judge dismissed the case. I gave the notebook to dear Ellen Doubleday as a memento, and all I can recollect, after that first visit to the States, was being seasick all the way home in the *Queen Mary*.

When, after many more visits to the Doubledays,

dearest Ellen died, she left the notebook to her daughter Puckie. Puckie returned it to me. And I reread it, for the first time in thirty years, when I received it.

And so I bring my *Rebecca* saga to an end. Perhaps the reader may care to compare it, and the original epilogue, with the published novel. If not, never mind!

THE REBECCA NOTEBOOK

Epilogue. Written.

Chapter I. A companion, sketch of early life. Father a doctor in Eastbourne, mother dead. Left with little money. Detail of companion's existence. Hotel dining room. Henry for the first time. The courtesy of H compared to other men.

Chapter II. Progress in friendship: drive perhaps somewhere, Manderley, descriptions. More of Henry. Asks her to marry him. And Mrs. Van Hopper, "My dear, you're a very lucky girl." (Mrs. V.H. had given her notice anyway, going back to America.) That's when she tells him all this before. "Don't flatter yourself he's in love with you, my dear. Poor fellow, he's incorrigibly lonely, like all widowers who can't forget their first wife. He practically told me as much."

Chapter III. Married, and so to Manderley. The house, the rooms, determined to do well. Mrs. Danvers, such opposition. "It is a little difficult, madam, for us. You see we were all very fond of Mrs. de Winter."

Chapter IV. Henry's sister, Barbara. Rather brusque, not unfriendly. Looks her up and down a bit. "You don't mind my saying so, but you ought to do something to your hair"— and then when she goes, "You're very different from Rebecca."

Chapter V. Atmosphere rather getting her down. And then the drive over to see the old grandmother. Deaf and rather senile. "Well, old lady, how are you?" Self anxious to please, and ill at ease. "Who are you, I don't know you, I haven't seen you before. Henry, who is this girl? I want Rebecca: where is my Rebecca? What have you done with Rebecca?" The nurse comes in, everyone stands up, awful embarrassment, "I think perhaps you had better go, rather too much excitement for her." Henry in the car very white and silent. "I'm so terribly sorry. I had no idea she would do that." "Don't be absurd, it's absolutely all right."

Chapter VI. Riding efforts, no good at all, Henry over-kind. The serving-woman, and the dress in the cupboard, Rebecca's. "How tall she must have been?" "Yes, m'm, she was, what you would call statuesque." The meet, the flashy loose-lipped cousin. Glance of derision. "I thought I'd pay my respects to your wife." Henry's anger. "Keep away from Manderley in future, do you hear? You dirty swine." They stared at one another. Self frightened and bewildered. Never seen Henry angry before. Looked upon something that she was not meant to see.

Chapter VII. The woodman, and the summerhouse. A bit senile too. "You're kind, and you've got gentle eyes. You're not like the other one." "The other one? Who do you mean?" He looked very sly, he laid his finger against his nose. "She used to come up here," he whispered, "I seen her with me own eyes. Be night she'd come, she'd not be alone. And then I run against her face to face. 'You've never seen me before, have you?' she said. 'No,' I said. 'And you'll not know me if you see me again, will you?' says she. 'No, ma'am,' says I. 'I'm not going to give you any money,' she says, 'but if you tell anyone you have seen me here I shall have you put to the asylum. You don't want

15

to go there, do you?' she says. 'No, ma'am,' I says, 'I don't want no harm to come to a living soul.' She's dead now, ain't she? Tall she was, and dark, she'd give you the feeling of a snake. Have you come to put me to the asylum too?" He was crazy, of course, poor old fellow, and yet—how puzzling his description. It was not one's idea of Rebecca.

(Must separate these two chapters by a more intimate depressing reaction. The coat under the stairs, the handkerchief in the pocket. Then the snapshot, Henry laughing, bending over her—I couldn't see her face. It was my favourite corner of the garden, where we had sat yesterday for tea, spoiling my memory. Mrs. Van Hopper had been right. "I can't see you mistress of a place like Manderley, somehow I feel you'll regret it." I felt now I had no right to be there. What had happened to those weeks, and days—nothing died, nothing was wasted. That moment, when Henry and Rebecca stood there, side by side, where had it gone? He was my husband and I knew nothing of him. Sitting in the library, staring in front of him. No sound but the clicking of my needles. Probably an irritation.)

Chapter VIII. The dance. Chooses a dress of one of the pictures. Doesn't tell Henry. It's to be a surprise. Great preparations. Looks very well. Goes to the head of the staircase and stands there. The sea of faces looking up. A hum. Then Henry, white-faced, his eyes blazing with anger. "What the hell do you think you're doing?" Pause, a hand on the banister. "It's the picture, the one in the drawing room." A deathly silence. "Go and change, at once. Put on an ordinary evening frock—anything, it doesn't matter what. We won't wait for you."

Back to the bedroom, the little maid crying, trembling fingers. Sat on the bed, twisting and turning her fingers. Knock on the door. Barbara comes in, swift and firm. "It's all right, my dear—put on anything, that charming white. I knew at once it was just a terrible mistake. You could not possibly have known."

"Known what?"

"Why, you poor silly child, that dress, the picture you copied, it was identical with the one Rebecca wore, the last fancy-dress dance at Manderley."

I sat stunned. "I ought to have known," stupidly over and over again. "I ought to have known."

"Of course Henry thought it was deliberate on your part —I said at once it was not, how could you have known? It was sheer bad luck you chose that particular picture."

"I can't go down now. I can't face them all."

"You must; if you don't they will all think you meant to do it. I'll explain everything. Just slip down in your white frock."

"No—Barbara, I can't. After dinner, I'll try."

Goes down and stands by his side in the hall. The interminable evening winds on. Henry, with set white face, does not speak to her at all. To bed, and he goes to his dressing-room.

Chapter IX.   The next morning. Aftermath of the ball. I could not face the guests. Sent a note down. And they all go away. Verbal message from Henry, "Gone up to London." The silence of the house. Potters through the woods, utterly lost and miserable. It should have been so different. Henry made a terrible mistake in marrying me, that's evident. He wanted to be alone with his memories, and I had intruded upon him and Rebecca. Mrs. Van Hopper had been right. I was making a mistake, she had said, "I don't think you'll be happy." Rebecca still dwelt in Manderley, and she resented me. Overwrought and hysterical. I went and unlocked the secret drawer in my desk. I took out the snapshot of Rebecca. I was very calm. I knew what she wanted me to do. It was as though she was sitting by my side. "We don't want you here, we don't want you. Henry wants to be alone with me."

I sat down at the desk and wrote to Henry. The letter. Then I went upstairs and took the bottle of Lysol from the bathroom cupboard.

Chapter X. The delirium, and here I can use the early bits if I like (unless already used), Eastbourne and the rest in disjointed form. That can be worked up. The beat of the metronome—*un deux, un deux, un deux,* and the burning of my throat. Yes, of course, it was the tar, the liquid tar that the men were pouring down my throat. "My darling, my darling, why in the name of God didn't you tell me? My beloved, my sweet." His hands and his voice, his hands pulling me back, his cheek against mine. "Of course she stood between us, of course I could not love you with her diabolical shadow haunting me, standing forever like a living threat. Don't you understand, darling, that I killed Rebecca, she was never drowned, that body that was washed up, that I identified, was not hers at all. I shot her that night in the cottage in the woods, I carried her vicious damnable body down to the boat—and laid it in the cabin. It was I who set sail, I who slipped the moorings, and when we were three miles out I opened the sea cocks, bored holes in the planking to make my work more swift—then, casting the life buoy over the side and the fenders and her oilskins to act as evidence, I jumped into the dinghy and pulled away. The boat sank in ten minutes. And Rebecca lies there now, ten fathoms deep, in the cabin of that little boat—and no one will ever know, my darling, no one will ever know."

Chapter XI. Recovered, on the lawn, tea and raspberries. Wood pigeons, the atmosphere entirely changed. Henry ten years younger. Rather a Menabilly-ish description.

Perhaps people to cricket. At any rate strike the peaceful note.

Chapter XII. Overcast summer day. Here perhaps the leaves blowing off the table. Sense of foreboding. They go indoors to escape a tropical shower. Leaves scatter fast. Feel there won't be tea on the lawn again. The last time. Later on rockets—go to the end of the lawn to see. Mist too thick.

Chapter XIII. Henry goes to London. Lonely without him. News of the wreck over breakfast. I go out to see her. She was about three miles offshore, a desolate-looking sight. Chat with an old fellow on the cliff. "They are going to send divers down, the cargo was valuable." They were rowing out in a boat even as I watched. The diver in his red-stockinged cap. Rather monotonous. Rather chilly. When I got back I found there was a telephone message from Henry, saying he would be back by the evening train.

Chapter XIV. Sitting quietly together in the library. Entrance of maid—the inspector. Twists his hat. I always liked Inspector Booth. "The divers came upon another wreck this afternoon, the wreck of a small sailing boat. Lying in fifteen fathom of water, sir. Do believe me, sir, I simply hate to come here and distress you, but from what they say the boat is unquestionably the late Mrs. de Winter's little *Gypsy*."

Chapter XV. Reactions of Henry—the pause—the tense atmosphere. He swallowed. "It was kind of you, Inspector, to come and tell me personally. I appreciate it very much." Discuss what is to happen. Leave it in peace perhaps. The inspector goes. So it was all to happen again, that shadow of Rebecca coming between us. And Henry, standing by

19

the window, "It's warm in here, isn't it?" His voice strained and unnatural. "My darling, I'm sorry, so desperately sorry." He did not answer. I went up to him and took his hand. "Just as we were forgetting her, just as we were beginning to be so happy." Still he did not move. It was unnatural. "What's the matter?" And then he broke down, like a child, I held out my arms to him and rocked him. "It's come at last, what I've dreamt about, what I have foreseen. This is the end of our brief happiness. You see —I killed Rebecca, and her dead body is lying in that cabin now."

Chapter XVI. The confession, she consoles him, they cling to each other. "We can't do anything until the morning."

Chapter XVII. Breakfast untasted. The glorious day. "Is it true Mrs. de Winter's boat has been found?" Mrs. Danvers, hungry, a ghoul scenting disaster. I was cold. "They are not sure." The telephone. We looked at each other. He went into the study and I followed him. The one-sided conversation. "Yes—yes, it's me speaking, Booth. Yes. Ah." I went out on to the terrace. Too good a morning. Unfair, and shameless. He came out. He took my hands. "They've found the body in the cabin of *Gypsy.* I'm going down right away."

Chapter XVIII. Waiting for him to return, it seemed hours. At last the sound of the car. I was sick with apprehension. He was not alone. Major Gray, the chief constable, was with him. Impossible to catch Henry alone. Goes to wash his hands. "This is a most distressing thing, Mrs. de Winter, I do feel for and your husband very acutely. It makes it all the more difficult, you see, your husband having identified that original body, over a year ago." "Then—then something was found in the cabin."

"Oh, yes," he lowered his voice, "it was her, without a doubt. Of course—the actual body was completely decomposed, you know—but the remains were sufficient for your husband to attest—" He stopped, Henry had come into the room. "Lunch is ready," he said briefly. "Shall we go in?" "I wish I could spare you the formality of an inquest," he said, "but I'm afraid it's impossible." Discuss it from every angle. He goes at last. Henry seemed calm now. "Everything will be all right. No one has any suspicion. It's simply a case of mistaken identity. That's all. I'm not afraid. How can I regret having killed Rebecca? I don't, I never have. There's never been one pang of remorse at that part of it. But it's you—marrying you under false pretences, dragging you through this." But she is with him.

Chapter XIX. The coroner's court. The witness of the diving and then Henry. Quite straightforward, though rather tricky about why the body was in the cabin. Henry skates well over thin ice. Then the member of the jury. The boat builder. A nasty little man. (Not really, I suppose.) "What I don't understand, sir, is this. I've been and looked at the little boat, I ought to know, it was my young nipper that built her. She was well built, strongly built, and where she was lying ten fathoms deep is just off the rocky ground. Now, what is the meaning of these holes drilled in the bows —that's never rocks that done that, nor natural corrosion of sea water. Them holes have been drilled with a vice and bit."

Chapter XX. The coroner suggests adjourning until the afternoon, for further evidence to be obtained. (Again Major Gray and the coroner to lunch.) Another wretched meal. Then the afternoon. The planks are produced. The boat builder's son has had time to make a full investigation. He goes in the box. "Yes, sir, these planks have been drilled right through. And there's one other thing,

sir, that I don't think was noticed. The sea cocks was turned full on." "I'm afraid I do not quite follow." "Why, sir,
the plug that brought water to the sink. They are closed
when an owner puts to sea. This one was full on, and what
with the holes drilled and this as well it wouldn't take long
for a small craft to sink. Not much above fifteen to twenty
minutes, sir. I built her, sir, and I was proud of my work,
and so was Mrs. de Winter. She was soundly built. It's my
opinion that the little craft was deliberately scuttled."
Sensation. "I see no alternative but to call Mr. de Winter
again." Apologises. "Can you suggest any reason for
this?" "It was shock enough to learn that I identified the
wrong body a year ago. Now it is thrust upon me that my
late wife was drowned in the cabin of her boat, and further-
more that the cabin was bored to let in the water. Are you
suggesting that this was done deliberately, by my wife, before sailing, and that she calmly sat in the cabin and watched the water pour through the floorboards?" The coroner
was nonplussed. "I realise this is very distressing for you,
and for Mrs. de Winter." I felt all eyes in my direction.
"But the evidence seems overwhelming. Mr. de Winter,
have you any reason to suspect that your late wife wished
to put an end to herself?" "None at all." "I think we had
better go into the facts of last year in rather more detail."
(Work this up when the time comes.) Getting more and
more exhausted. The atmosphere stifling. A note handed
to the coroner. He looked up like a stuffed owl, over his
spectacles. "There is someone here who wishes to give evidence. Mr. Paul Astley, please."

Chapter XXI. It was the loose-lipped cousin. Henry
looked very tired. He is questioned. The cousin. "Quite
impossible for Mrs. de Winter to have committed suicide.
She was not the type, and certainly would never have
chosen the manner. If her husband suggests so I say he is
being deliberately misleading. Mrs. de Winter wrote me a

letter the evening she died. Here it is. I should like the letter to be read aloud. 'H going to London tomorrow night. Come to the cottage and discuss plans. Have a far better alternative to Paris—Rebecca.' " "What do you wish the jury to infer from this?" "It's quite simple, isn't it? Mrs. de Winter and I were in love with each other. She was going to leave her husband. We had thought of flying to Paris. But in that note she asks me to meet her in the old wood-man's cottage at Manderley, to discuss plans. You see the note was written at nine-fifteen. Would she have written that and gone straight off and committed suicide?"

"Mr. Astley, was Mr. de Winter aware of the relations between you and his wife?'

'Of course he was, ask him, he can't deny it."

"Do you imply that he shut his eyes to the fact?"

"No, he was madly jealous. She often told me so."

"Did you understand he was ignorant of this Paris plan?"

"As far as I knew he was ignorant. But it is quite within the bounds of possibility that she told him that evening, that they had a row, and that he, in one of his stinking rages, plugged holes in that boat knowing that it would sink. Go on, ask him, ask him to prove that he's innocent, can't you—ask him to prove it!"—the terrible white look on Henry's face—that terrible white lost look.

The evidence is overwhelming. Leads up to the question, "Then, Mr. de Winter, you never at any time had a suspicion that your wife might do away with herself?" (Overwhelming relief, because it looked all the time as though they were working up to a leading question on murder.) "Will somebody take my wife home? She is going to faint." I think it was little Dr. Marsden who caught my hands as I fell. End of chapter.

Chapter XXII. Back home. Sits in a sort of stupor. Henry returns. Aged, and very tired. Verdict of suicide, without sufficient evidence to show the state of mind of the deceased. "We'll have to get away." "Won't it look suspicious?" "Let's go away this evening, Henry, quietly, to some stodgy respectable hotel in London, where no one will know us, where we are just two people out of eight million." "Yes—" very wearily, "yes." "We had better go away tonight then?" "No, not tonight." "Why not?" "Because something has to be done first. It was Gray who suggested this evening. If we do it in the day there might be a morbid crowd of sightseers. I've arranged for it to be tonight at half past nine." "Yes, of course, I understand." It was though Rebecca had died but yesterday. There was that particular atmosphere about the house connected with the aftermath of death. A sort of standing by—marking of time. Mrs. Danvers. She had been crying. "Please, Mr. de Winter, I understand Mrs. de Winter is to be buried this evening. With your permission I should like to be present. She was always very good to me." I wondered why she looked at Henry like that, an unfathomable question in her eyes. "Yes, Mrs. Danvers, of course, I appreciate your wish. You understand, though, the ceremony is to be entirely private. There will be no one attending but myself. I must ask you to say nothing about it to the servants." "They none of them know, sir." "Very well, then." We did not talk much during dinner. When he had gone I went upstairs to pack. I felt that I was doing things for the last time. When the stable clock struck ten, its odd high-pitched note, it seemed to me that I would not hear it again. Packing rather mechanically, and then the knock on the door. "Do you know how long Mr. de Winter will be?" "I don't suppose he'll be much after half past ten. Why?" "Mr. Paul Astley is below, and wants to see him."

Chapter XXIII. She has a short interview with him first. "You know what has happened, of course? I don't know that Henry will see you. All this has been very upsetting, and we are going away." He kept examining his nails, and there was something about his half-smile that I did not like. "Going away. Yes, I think that's very wise of you. Gossip is an unpleasant thing, and it's always more pleasant to avoid it."

"I don't think we are going for that reason."

"No? Of course, it's been a great shock to me. Rebecca was my second cousin, you know, I was devoted to her." Work up the scene. And then Henry returns.

"What are you doing here?" "Well, actually I came to offer my congratulations."

"Do you mind leaving the house; or do you prefer to be chucked out?"

"Steady a moment, Henry. You've done very well out of this affair. You realise of course that I can make things extremely unpleasant for you, I might almost say dangerous?" I gripped the arms of my chair. Henry was unmoved. He lit a cigarette. The evidence is torn to shreds, the copy of the note is produced. "If this was made public, if I told my full story—damn the consequences to my reputation—it would put a very different light on the affair wouldn't it?" "Well, what do you propose to do? There's the telephone. Ring up Gray and tell him your story."

"Wait a bit, wait a bit. No need to get rattled. I'm a poor man, Henry, I don't want to smash you up. Why don't we come to an agreement? Here, I'll put all my cards on the table. Let me have a settlement of two thousand a year and I swear to God I'll never trouble you again." "Get out." "No, wait," I said. I turned swiftly to Paul Astley. "I see what you're driving at. It happens, by some devilish stroke of ill fortune, that things could be twisted round to make it very difficult for Henry. Perhaps he does not see it as clearly as I do. I think we ought to consider this offer of yours." "Don't you interfere with this. Don't you see that it's blackmail? Give him two thousand a year for life?" "It depends how much you value your own. Mrs. de

Winter doesn't fancy being pointed at as the widow of a murderer, a fellow who was hanged, do you?"

"You think you can blackmail me, Astley, but you're wrong." Very white. "I'm not afraid of anything you can do. There's the telephone. Shall I ring up Gray, ask him to come over?"

"You would not dare. This evidence is enough to hang you." Henry walked to the telephone. "Give me Cutty 17, please." I saw our safety fall from us piece by piece. Rings Gray. "Will you come along here?" Gray comes. "Good evening, Henry. What's happened?" "You know Paul Astley, Rebecca's cousin." "Yes, we have met, I think." "Very well, Astley, go ahead." (Wind out of sails.) "Look here, Gray, I'm not satisfied with the verdict." "Isn't that for de Winter to say?"

"No, I don't think it is. I have a right to speak, not only as Rebecca's cousin but, if she had lived, as her prospective husband."

"Is this true, Henry?" Henry laughed shortly.

"So he says, Arthur, if you want to believe it you can."

"Supposing you tell me exactly what's wrong."

"Listen here, Gray, this note was written to me half an hour before Rebecca was supposed to have set out on that suicidal sail. Here it is, I want you to say whether you think a woman who wrote that note had made up her mind to kill herself?"

"No—on the face of it, no. What does the note refer to? What were these plans?"

"We were going to Paris. It was her idea, she loathed Manderley, loathed every stick and stone in the place. Henry was going to London, it was an escapade after her own heart."

" 'I've got something to tell you.' What do you suppose that means?"

"I don't know. One never knew with Rebecca. It might mean anything. But there was the meeting—nine-thirty—

in the cottage, it's as plain to me as though she was standing here now."

"What are you suggesting, get done with these insinuations and speak out."

'Rebecca never plugged the holes in that boat, Gray, Rebecca never committed suicide, she was murdered, and if you want to know who the murderer is, why there he is —standing there with his God damned superior smile, he couldn't even wait till the year was out before marrying again, the first chit of a girl he set his eyes on—there's your murderer for you, Mr. Henry de Winter of Manderley." He began to laugh, high-pitched and foolish, the laugh of a drunkard, and all the while pointing his finger at Henry, who stood very still in his corner by the window.

Chapter XXIV. They go into it more carefully. "You say you were Mrs. de Winter's lover. Can you prove it? Have you other letters? I want to remind you of this, because in a court of law you might find yourself making a big mistake." (Henry interposes about the blackmail.) "No, I didn't. Rebecca was not the sort of woman to write love letters."

"Does anybody know?"

"Yes—there's one person knows. But whether she'd speak the truth or not I don't know. But she might speak, if she thought it would help Rebecca." Already I had an inkling of what was to come.

"Well, who is it?"

"Mrs. Danvers."

"Then I think the simplest thing to do would be to ask Mrs. Danvers to come here."

Mrs. Danvers comes. Tall and gaunt. She had evidently been weeping.

"Mrs Danvers, were you aware of the relationship between the late Mrs. de Winter and Mr. Astley?"

"They were second cousins, so I've always understood."

27

"No—I was not referring to blood relationship. Were you aware that there existed a closer relationship than that?"

"I don't understand you." Astley laughed coarsely.

"Come off it, Mrs. Danvers. You knew damn well that Mrs. de Winter and I (etc., etc.). I've already told Major Gray, but he won't believe me. Come now, admit what you know, she was in love with me, wasn't she?"

Mrs. Danvers considered him a moment. I can't describe her smile, it had all the meaning of disdain and scorn.

"She was not."

"Listen here, Mrs. Danvers—"

"She was not in love with you, no, nor with her husband. She was above you all, she despised all men."

"Look here—didn't she creep down the woodland path to me at nights, weren't you waiting up for her sometimes, didn't she spend nights with me in London?"

"Well"—with sudden passion—"what if she did, hadn't she a right to amuse herself the way she liked? Love-making was a game with her, she told me often, she did it because it made her laugh, it made her laugh, I tell you," etc., etc., torrent of passion.

It was horrible, unexpected, and it was not helping Henry.

"Can you suggest any reason why she should have taken her life?"

"No—I've lain awake at nights, Major Gray, reproaching myself. If I'd been at Manderley that night."

"You were not here?"

"No—I'd gone into Sudbury. I usually went on Friday afternoons, and I missed my bus. I didn't get back till after nine. She had gone then." I felt pity for Mrs. Danvers now. If only that loyalty was ours.

"Mrs. Danvers, you knew Mrs. de Winter very well, we can gather that from what you've already told us." Astley would have spoken but he motioned him to be quiet. "Can you think of any reason, however remote, why Mrs. de Winter should have taken her own life?" She shook her head slowly. "No," she said, "no, Major Gray. Ever since the verdict I've been thinking about it, turning it over and over in my mind."

"There you see," Astley said swiftly, "it's impossible, I've told you that."

"Be quiet, Astley," he thundered, "give Mrs. Danvers time to think. If we'd known how she'd spent her day in London it might help."

"She had a hair appointment from twelve till one-thirty. She lunched alone at her club, and came down by train about half past three."

"It ought to be easy to verify that. What was she doing from two until three."

"Wait—I've got her engagement diary. You know you let me have all those little mementoes, when she went. They're locked in my room. Everything she did she'd write down, and tick off with an X."

Goes to fetch it. "Yes—here it is—'Hair 12.00. Lunch at Club. 2 o'clock. Baker.' "

"Who's Baker?"

"Baker, Baker. Never heard of the fellow."

"Baker. I don't know the name. But look here, she's put a great X after that, as though as a special gesture. I believe if we knew who Baker was we'd be near to solving Mrs. de Winter's suicide. Mrs. Danvers, she wasn't in the hands of moneylenders?" "No." "Blackmailers?" A glance at Astley. Too careful for that. "She had no enemy, no one she was in fear of?"

"Mrs. de Winter afraid? She was afraid of no one and nobody, there was only one thing that she was afraid of— and that was pain."

We all of us stared. Paul Astley looked astonished.

"What on earth do you mean? What about the falls she had out hunting? What about the dogs she looked after?"

"Not that sort of pain, Mr. Paul. She was, like all strong people, afraid of being ill, and most of all of having operations. 'When I die, Danny,' she said to me, 'I hope it will be quick, like the snuffing of a candle. If I knew I was to suffer—I think I'd go clear off my head.'"

That seems no good.

"That's why I was glad it was a quick death. They say drowning is painless, don't they?" Eagerly. I felt sorry for Mrs. Danvers. At any rate, I thought, Henry and I both knew that Rebecca had died painlessly.

"When did she say that?"

"She always felt that way, all the time I knew her. But she did say it to me not long before she died."

"What in hell's the use of all this, we're getting away from the point all the time. Baker, if we only knew." Mrs. Danvers had been going through the diary. Suddenly, she gave an exclamation. "There's something here, right at the back, between a number of loose pages. Baker—and the number 1057. That's the telephone number. No exchange, though."

"Try all the London exchanges with that number. It will take you a week. What's the time?" (Make it earlier.) I could see that Henry, like the rest of us, considered the tracing of Baker a wild goose chase. However, it served to delay. It might quieten Gray for the time.

"This will cost you a bit. [Explain about telephone books.] Give us this book again. Is that a dash after the number? Couldn't it, with a little ingenuity, be twisted into M?" He tries one number, etc. Couple named Carter lived there for seven years. "Try Museum, sir," from Mrs. Danvers. He does so. Night porter. Anyone named Baker. "No, sir, I've only been here six months. There may have been. I believe there was a gentleman of that name once."

"Could you inform me, is it a private house or offices? Ah—" He turned, an odd, rather triumphant look in his eyes. "The man said he believed there was a man named Baker there once and it's not offices."

"What are they?" from Astley.

"The address is 113 Harley Street, and are a number of doctors' consulting rooms." Then I knew at once. Of course Rebecca spent the hour from two to three with the doctor who had told her that, etc.

Chapter XXV. Journey to London to Harley St. Baker of course retired six months ago through ill-health. Living in Hampstead. Trek to Hamp—(noose drawing tighter round his neck). Baker out when they get there. They sit round the room, description of, etc. Baker comes in. Different somehow. Gray takes the initiative, and asks the question. On the thirteenth of last year, between two and three, a Mrs. de Winter.

Shakes his head, no idea of the name.

Perhaps she did not come under her own name. Here, he looks up his diary. "I see a Mrs. Winter booked an appointment for that day. Hold on, I'll go through my files. Yes— here we are. H'm. Yes—of course you know, unprofessional conduct."

"This is Mr. de Winter. In strict confidence, she committed suicide, we strongly believe, and it is possible, just possible, you may furnish us with the motive." I waited for his denial, for his inevitable, "Mrs. Winter, if I remember rightly, did not strike me as being the sort of woman who would be afraid to have a child." But instead he glanced through his files again. "She had been to have some X rays taken, and she came to know the results. She told me, 'I want to know the truth, no gentle bedside manner for me.' She had a deep-rooted malignant growth, and since she had asked for the truth I let her have it. The pain was slight as yet, but in six months' time, perhaps in less than that, she would have to be under morphia. An operation might have done some good, personally I believe not."

"Dr. Baker," Henry leaning forward, "you are quite certain of this? There is no possibility of mistake?"

"None at all. Outwardly Mrs. Winter was a perfectly healthy woman. There was a certain malformation of the u, she could never have had a child, for instance, but that had nothing to do with the disease."

We sat silent. It was Arthur Gray who first rose to his feet. "I think Dr. Baker has told us all we wanted to know. If you could let us have a copy of that analysis."

"Oh, certainly."

We went outside.

"I think you two had better go off on your own," he said. "I'll deal with Astley. This"—he tapped the document—"and Mrs. Danvers' statement give us our motive. There's no twisting about of that. And blackmail is a very ugly charge. You can leave it all to me."

He hailed a taxi. "God bless you both," he said abruptly. And then he was gone. We got into the car.

"He knows, of course," said Henry.

"Yes," I said.

And we went along the North Circular Road, etc., etc.

Chapter XXVI. Going towards Manderley. We still have to go away—they take the decision, they go over it all. After all that has happened. Perhaps Rebecca will have the last word yet. The road narrows before the avenue. A car with blazing headlights passed. Henry swerved to avoid it, and it came at us, rearing out of the ground, its huge arms outstretched to embrace us, crashing and splintering above our heads.

Epilogue?

1 Atmosphere.
2 Simplicity of style.
3 Keep to the main theme.
4 Characters few and well defined.
5 Build it up little by little.

THE REBECCA EPILOGUE

If you travel south you will come upon us in the end, staying in one of those innumerable little hotels that cling like
limpets to the Mediterranean shore. You will be passing
through to somewhere more attractive, but we are fixtures
there, and have been for many months. As you walk into
the dining room you will not notice us at first, for we have
a table in the corner by the window; but when you have
eaten your inevitable hors d'oeuvre, and are considering
the plate of roast veal and haricot beans that the obliging
but clumsy little waiter has put before you, you will hear
my voice for a moment, raised above the clatter of plates,
demanding a bottle of Evian water in ineffectual French.
You groan inwardly, and hope that we will not edge into
conversation with you when the time comes to take coffee
in the lounge. The nuisance is spared to you, however, for
when *déjeuner* is over we make for the shady side of the
verandah without glancing once in your direction.

You see then that he is crippled, he walks slowly and
awkwardly with the aid of sticks, and it is some little time
before I have settled him for the afternoon. There is the
long chair to adjust, the pillows to arrange, and the rug
over his knees; and when this is done to his satisfaction,
and he has rewarded me with a smile, I sit down beside
him and open my bag of knitting.

You watch us covertly for a while from behind the concealing pages of the continental *Daily Mail*, and speculate
idly upon our identity. His face is vaguely familiar to you.
There is something arresting about his profile and the line
of his jaw, but it is impossible to put a name to him. Of

course there are replicas of us all over Europe. Both of us bear upon our persons the unmistakable signs of the wandering English who live abroad.

He very immaculate, with fresh linen, smelling of eau de cologne and bath salts, a copy of *The Times* on his lap, his panama hat set at just the right angle, and I with faded hair and colouring, dark glasses concealing eyes that have lost their brightness, and upon my rather dumpy body one of an unending series of cotton frocks, too long for me and sagging at the hem. Later in the day you run up against me in the English library, the bag of knitting still under one arm and three books under the other, and as I pass you I leave a little whiff of lavender water in my wake. I dab it on with the stopper behind each ear every morning, and it lasts me for the day.

During your brief visit you notice that we live very much by routine. The chairs are put out on the verandah after breakfast and we stay there, with intervals for meals, until sundown. Sometimes I wander off for walks alone, carrying a cardigan I have knitted myself and a local walking stick with a spike at the bottom, but I am always back in time for tea. He has had a nap whilst I was gone, and wakes just in time for my return, preceded by the little waiter with tea. We shift with the sun, and when the first chill of evening falls upon the verandah I put a marker in the book I have been reading to him, and start the small task of getting him indoors. You gather that changing for dinner at half past seven is rather a business for us, but nevertheless we appear in the nick of time, he faultless as usual and reminding you once again of some familiar face, and I in black lace with a fur round my shoulders. We keep very much to ourselves, and beyond a courteous good morning and good night to the few other inhabitants of the hotel, and a more genuine smile to the staff, you never see us talk to anyone.

The day come for you to leave for your more exciting

rendezvous. This spot is deadly dull, of course, but the rest has done you good, and as you stand on the verandah for the last time, waiting for your luggage to come down, you see us sitting in our usual corner of the verandah, sipping our midmorning coffee. Something prompts you to walk across and say good-bye. You come upon us unawares, and for the first time you notice that there is an indefinable air of sadness about us, a sort of aftermath of tragedy, and you feel a little uncomfortable, as though you had clumsily stumbled against a barrier. You are saved from embarrassment by our smiles, and there is nothing tragic in the way we wish you bon voyage, and chat for a moment quite pleasantly about your destination. We both look rather hungrily at your luggage, and the thought comes to you, very surprisingly, that perhaps we wish we were going too.

"Are you making a long stay here?" you ask; and I pause a moment before replying, throwing him a glance, "Our plans are rather indefinite," leaving it at that. The stout hall porter has assembled your luggage and is waiting for his tip. There is nothing to delay you now.

"Well, so long," you say, "we shall probably meet at home some day."

The Englishman shakes your hand and wishes you good luck. "No," he says, half to you, half to himself, "no, we shall never go home again."

And then, you smile, and wave, and disappear round the corner of the verandah. You think about us vaguely when you get into the train. Why do they do it, you wonder; leading apparently aimless lives? For what purpose? Are they really in quest of the sun, or is their existence a way of escape, from something or someone?

We shall never live in England again, that much is certain. The past would be too close to us. Those things we are trying to forget and put behind us would stir again, and that sense of fear, of furtive unrest struggling at length to master unreasoning panic—now mercifully stilled, thank God—might in some manner unforeseen become a living companion, as it did before. We are not unhappy, that I would impress upon you. Henry at least knows something of the peace of God, which, poor darling, he never possessed before. He is wonderfully patient and never complains, not even when he is in pain, which happens, I think, rather more often than he would have me know. I can tell by the way he will look puzzled suddenly, and lost, all expression dying away from his dear face as though swept by an unseen hand, and in its place a mask will form, a sculptured thing, formal and cold, beautiful still but lifeless. He will fall to smoking cigarette after cigarette, not bothering to extinguish them, and the glowing stubs will lie around him on the ground like petals. He will talk quickly and eagerly about nothing at all, an unusual thing for such a silent person, snatching at any subject, however trivial, as a panacea to pain.

I remember my father expounding once upon the theory that men and women emerge stronger and finer after suffering, and that to advance in this or any world we must endure ordeal by fire. He should have known, of course— he was a doctor. And I, at the time a chubby schoolgirl in tearing health from a scramble on the south downs, considered it a dreary doctrine. Since then I have known fear, and loneliness, and very great distress. I have watched my beloved husband come through a great crisis, and I—I was not a silent spectator. I know now that it is not easy to live. Sooner or later, in the life of everyone comes a moment of trial. We all of us have our own particular devil who rides us and torments us, and we must give battle in the end. Henry and I have conquered ours, or so we believe. The devil does not ride us any more. But we are shorn of our little earthly glory, he a cripple and his home lost to him, and I, well, I suppose I am like all childless women, craving for echoes I shall never hear, and lacking a certain quality of tenderness. Like a ranting actress in an indifferent play, I might say that this is the price we have to pay for our freedom. But I have had enough of melodrama in this life, and would bereave my Henry of his five senses if it would ensure him his present peace and security until eternity.

As I said before, we are not unhappy. We have money to live without discomfort. Granted that the little hotel you found us in was cheap, the food indifferent, and that day after day dawns very much the same, yet we would not have it otherwise. We both appreciate simplicity, and if we are sometimes bored—well, boredom is a pleasing antidote to fear. The only time Henry shows impatience is when the postman lags, for it means we must wait perhaps another day before hearing the result of some match played a week ago. We have tried wireless, but the noise is such an irritant, and we prefer to store up our excitement against the arrival of our mail. Oh, the Test Matches that have saved us from ennui, the boxing bouts, even the billiard scores. Finals of schoolboy sports, dog racing, strange little competitions in the remoter counties, all these are grist to our hungry mill. Sometimes old copies of the *Field* come our way, and I am transported from this indifferent shore to the reality of an English spring. I read of chalk streams and the mayfly, of harbours where the tide is at the flood, of sorrel growing in meadows, and rooks circling above church towers as they used to do at Manderley. The smell of wet earth comes to us from those thumbed and tattered pages, the sour tang of moorland peat, and handful upon handful of green and soggy moss, spattered white in places with the herons' droppings.

Once there was an article on wood pigeons, and as I read it aloud to Henry it was as though I was once again in the deep woods at Manderley, the pigeons fluttering above my

head. I heard their soft complacent call, so comfortable
and cool on a hot summer's afternoon, and there would be
no disturbing of their peace until Jasper came loping
through the bracken to find me, his damp muzzle questing
the ground, his spaniel ears a-droop, his jowl saggy, and
his great eyes a perpetual reproach. Then like old ladies
caught at their ablutions, the bathroom door ajar, the
pigeons would flutter from their hiding place, shocked into
silly agitation, and making a monstrous to-do with their
wings streak away from us above the treetops, and so out
of sight and sound. While I, yawning idly, would recollect
that the sun by now had left the rose garden, there were
languid heads upon lean stalks calling for water, but most
important of all there were fresh raspberries for tea . . . .

It was the grey look on Henry's face that made me stop
abruptly and turn the pages until I found an article on
cricket, very practical and dull. Middlesex batting on a
hard wicket at the Oval, piling up interminable dreary
runs—how I blessed their stolid flannelled figures—and in
a few minutes his face had settled back into repose, the
colour had returned, and he was deriding the Surrey bowling in healthy irritation. We were saved a retreat into the
past and I had learnt my lesson. That grey look meant
hunger and regret, and bitterness too for this exile we had
brought upon ourselves, so in future I must keep away
from colour and scent and sound, rain and the lapping of
water. Read English news, yes, and English sport, politics
and pomposity, but keep the things that hurt to myself
alone. They can be my secret indulgence.

Some people have a vice for reading Bradshaws, and
plan innumerable journeys across country for fun of link-
ing up impossible connections. I, on the contrary, am a
mine of information on the English countryside. I know
the name of every owner of every British moor, and their
tenants too. I know how many partridge are killed on

such-and-such an estate, how many pheasants, how many head of deer. I know where trout are rising, and where salmon are leaping; even the names of those who are walking hound puppies are familiar to me. I attend all meets, I follow every run. The state of the crops, the price of fat cattle, the mysterious ailments of pigs. I relish them all. A poor pastime, perhaps, and not a very intellectual one, but I breathe the air of England as I read, and can face this glittering sky with greater courage.

That afternoon you saw me set forth upon my walk, stick in hand, was passed by me in the west country on a misty afternoon. I did not notice the scrubby vineyards and the crumbling stones because I was picking foxgloves and campion from a wet streaking hedge. Yes, I know my cotton frock sagged at the back, and my cardigan had stretched, and I came back worn and dusty-looking. I noticed your pitying, indulgent smile. For all that I had enjoyed my afternoon, and it was worth being away from Henry to find his smile of welcome when I returned.

Although you were hiding behind the *Daily Mail* I know you were watching the little ritual of our tea. The order never varies. Two slices of bread and butter each, one Indian tea, one China (I take mine with lemon), and two brioches with apricot jam. No cake. Henry has a theory that it gives him indigestion. What a hidebound, pernickety couple we must seem to an outsider like yourself, clinging to our routine and living like slaves to the clock. Having a sit-down tea at half past four because we always did in England. You should have seen us at Manderley— there it was even more of a ritual. In winter we had it in the library, the table put within comfortable distance of the roaring log fire. On the stroke of the half hour old Robert would fling open the door, followed by that nervous young footman he was in the process of training, who will never become proficient until he can control his hands from shaking, and the performance of laying the table would be carried out under the forbidding eye of Robert, who now and again communicated with his minion by way of dumb show.

Such a feast would be laid before us always, and yet we ate so little, Henry faithful always to his slice of bread and butter and his apricot jam. I must admit I went a little further. Those dripping crumpets, I can taste them now, alternating with piping-hot floury scones and tiny crisp wedges of toast. Sandwiches of a delectable but unknown nature, mysteriously flavoured, and that very special gingerbread. Angel cake that melted in the mouth, and its rather stodgier companion, bursting with peel and raisins. There must have been enough food there to keep a starving family for a week. I never knew what happened to it all. The waste used to worry me sometimes, but I never dared ask Mrs. Danvers what she did about it. She would have looked at me in scorn and smiled that freezing superior smile of hers. I can hear her say, "There were never any complaints when Mrs. de Winter was alive," before she swept away, leaving me standing on one foot. Poor Mrs. Danvers, I wonder what she is doing now. She always despised me. I think it was the expression on her face that gave me my first feeling of unrest. Instinctively I thought, "She is comparing me with Rebecca," and sharp as a sword the shadow came between us.

Well, it is over now, finished and done with. I ride no more tormented, and Henry is free. Even my faithful Jasper has gone to the happy hunting ground, and this summer Manderley opens as a country club. The prospectus was sent to me the other day. I did not show it to Henry, but put it away in the bottom of my trunk. They have demolished the old gun room and the flower room in the east wing, and my little morning room, and have built what they call a "sun loggia," Italian style, with vita glass,

41

so that the guests can sprawl about in negligée and acquire the fashionable tan.

Four concrete squash courts stand where the stables used to be, and they have sunk a swimming pool in the wilderness. The rose garden is a rose garden still, but they have discovered its possibilities for tea, and with gay little tables and bright umbrellas intend luring their clients there on summer afternoons. I have no doubt that Joe Allan and his Boys will look very well in the minstrels' gallery, so appropriately placed for their convenience above the great hall, where I gather the Saturday dances are to be held. Apparently the golf course will not be ready until the winter, for the park does not lend itself easily to conversion, and there are so many trees to come down. The place will be packed for the opening weekend, every room is booked already, and a famous film star is to start the proceedings by diving into the swimming pool in evening dress. The dress no doubt to be auctioned afterwards. Whether the venture is a success or not, one thing at least is certain. The guests will sleep soundly in their beds. Our ghosts will never trouble them. I shall keep the prospectus, though, and use it now and again as a lash when I fail in humour. It might stimulate in me an affection for cactus bushes and olive groves, stony vineyards and dusty bougainvillea.

And you, perhaps you will visit Manderley, one weekend, jaded and out of sorts from your London season. The west country is not so far in these days of easy flying, and they are sure to clear a landing ground for planes somewhere in the park. If you are stouthearted and not overburdened with imagination you can walk anywhere in Manderley with impunity, but if London life has put a strain upon your nerves there are one or two places I should avoid. The deep woods, for instance, after dark, and the little woodman's cottage. Here there may linger still a certain atmosphere of stress. That corner in the drive too, where the stump of a tree encroaches upon the gravel, it is not a spot in which to pause. Your fancy might play odd tricks upon you, especially when the sun has set. When the leaves rustle they sound very much like the stealthy movement of a woman in evening dress, and when they shiver suddenly, and fall and scatter before you on the ground, they could be the patter-patter of a woman's hurrying footstep, and that mark in the gravel the imprint of a high-heeled satin shoe.

No, if I were you I should toy with my cocktail in the new American bar, that billiard room always lacked atmosphere; and remain downstairs where you can hear the crooner braying, do not wander alone along the passages upstairs. There is a moment, just after twilight, if the moon is full, when the light streams through that long narrow window in the old west wing; and you could swear that in the corner there, against the door, where the shadows are darkest, there is a figure crouching, a woman surely. But perhaps the west wing is ablaze with electric light now, and dressing rooms and shower baths abound, and all the shadows have been swept away.

As you stand in the doorway of the hall, waiting for Joe Allan to strike up with one of his hot numbers, and light a cigar feeling at peace with yourself and the world, you will never connect Manderley with that fellow in the chaise longue and the panama hat, and his dull little wife in her faded cotton frock; yet it was not so long ago that Henry stood where you are standing now, whistling and calling to the dogs, and the step that you have sprinkled so freely with the ash from your cigar was thick with the crumbs I had scattered for the linnets . . . .

I suppose we are both very changed. Henry looks much older, of course, and his hair has gone very grey; but there is a certain stillness about him, an air of tranquillity that

was not there before, and I—rather too late in the day—
have lost my diffidence, my timidity, my shyness with
strangers. Perhaps Henry's dependence upon me for every
little thing has made me confident and bold at last. At any
rate I am different from that self who drove to Manderley
for the first time, hopeful and eager, handicapped by a
rather desperate gaucherie, and filled with an intense
desire to please. Those preceding years of companionship
with Mrs. Van Hopper had scarcely engendered in me
great qualities of confidence, and it was my lack of poise
that made such a bad impression on people like Mrs.
Danvers. What must I have seemed like after Rebecca . . .?

As we sit today at our table in the window, quietly working our way through from hors d'oeuvre to dessert, I think
of that other hotel dining room, larger and far more splendid than this, that dreadful Côte d'Azur at Monte Carlo,
and how, instead of having Henry opposite me, his steady,
well-shaped hands peeling a mandarin in methodical
fashion, I had Mrs. Van Hopper, her fat bejewelled fingers
questing a plate heaped with ravioli, her small pigs' eyes
darting suspiciously from her plate to mine for fear I
should have made a better bargain.

Only a few years ago—far fewer than you would suppose
—she dominated my small world; the salary she paid me
was one hundred and fifty pounds a year, and Manderley
was unknown to me. There was I, with straight bobbed
hair and youthful unpowdered face, trailing in her wake
like a subdued mouse. Now, with Henry by my side, in
spite of all we have lost, in spite of his maimed body and
scarred hands, those days, the terror, the distress, are
over, and I feel a glow of contentment come upon me. His
maimed body and my disfigurement are things of no
account, we have learned to accept them, we live, we
breathe, we have vitality, the spark of divinity has not
passed us by. This factor alone should be enough for us;

we have been spared to one another, and because of this we shall endure.

Déjeuner is over. The little waiter wipes the last crumbs from our table, and when I have helped Henry to his feet we make our usual pilgrimage to the verandah. The sun has lost its morning brilliance and is streaking to the west, leaving an afterglow which is easier to bear. Henry draws the rug over his knees, throws away his cigarette, then closes his eyes. I fix my dark glasses, reach for my bag of knitting. And before us, long as the skein of wool I wind, stretches the vista of our afternoon.

MEMORIES

INTRODUCTION

The eleven prose pieces which follow are not articles in the strict sense of the word, for I have never been a journalist but a writer of novels, stories and biographies, including one book of childhood and adolescent memoirs.

The fiction arose out of the unconscious, coupled with observation but above all with imagination. The pieces in the present section have nothing to do with my imagination, but with the conscious self, the person who is Me. This may sound, and probably is, conceited, but I make no apology for it; they were written at different times throughout my life because I felt strongly about the various subjects, and so was impelled to put my thoughts on paper.

The first three are about my grandfather, my father and my cousins, and I place them at the beginning because my family counted tremendously when I was young and as I matured, and still does in the latter half of my life. The only apology here is that I have not, as yet, written about my own children and my seven grandchildren.

The next three, again written at varying times throughout my professional career, express what I felt about three very different subjects, and here the reader may sense a certain cynicism of outlook which reflected my attitude to those matters at that particular moment. It is possible that my outlook has changed, perhaps developed, but this is not for me to say, because I cannot be sure.

"Death and Widowhood" was written with deep sincerity and emotion, coupled with a desire to help others who have suffered in similar fashion.

The last four follow in chronological order, the first of them describing how I found the house which was the setting for *Rebecca*. They bring the reader and myself up to date. Have I changed, matured, or sunk into senility? It is for the reader, not for myself, to judge!

THE YOUNG GEORGE DU MAURIER

[1951]

When George du Maurier died in October 1896, at the age of sixty-two, he was mourned not only by his family and his friends but by a wide circle of people who had come to know him through his drawings and his novels, and who felt, although they had never met him, that here was an artist and a writer who had expressed for many years all the graces of the world they knew. If the characters that he drew and wrote about were a little larger than life—the men almost too tall, the women more than beautiful—this was seen not as a fault but as a virtue; for du Maurier was a man who worshipped beauty and was not ashamed to put his ideals upon paper, which was something that his generation understood.

To him, as to his contemporaries, beauty was an end in itself. Whether it was the turn of a woman's head, her smooth dark hair parted in the centre with the low knot behind, and the curve of her shoulder; or the way a man stood, the way his shoulders were set; the sudden smile of a child, and the quiet, grave patience of old people—these were things to be revered and loved, and later reproduced with tenderness. Even when pulling jokes and poking fun —and as a humorous draughtsman for nearly thirty years he had a full measure of this—du Maurier was never malicious or unkind. He mocked at many, but with a twinkle in the eye. Never from him the sneer, the acid half-truth behind an innuendo, the damning Judas-thrust that passes for modern wit. He laughed at people because he loved them, because he understood and shared their little weaknesses, their foibles; their snobbery was his snobbery, their sudden social gaffes and faux pas were misfortunes committed all too often by himself, a bohemian at heart on the fringe of high society. The mistress of the house caught unexpectedly in disarray by unwelcome callers; the precocious child who faces a visitor with great innocent eyes and lets fall a blast of candour; the odd man out at a dinner party far above his milieu, the one cricketer among musicians, the one musician among cricketers, the bore who talks too much, the dullard who talks too little, the woman who laughs too loudly and too long—all these were targets for his pencil in those pages of *Punch* some sixty and seventy years ago, and no one appreciated the fact more than the delighted butts who recognised themselves.

It was the fashion once to decry the late Victorians, their pictures and their novels. They seemed hidebound and intolerant to a later age that promised freedom. Not so to-day. We have learnt our lesson. Looking back, separated from them by more than half a century, the years they graced and the world they delighted in appear to us now as things lovely and precious, lost by our own fault. I do not mean the mere picture postcard charm of crinolines and carriages, which du Maurier drew with his pencil and saw with his own eyes. Nor the lamplight that he knew, and the unbusy streets. Nor the houses new-painted for a London season, the window boxes gay, and the water cart that came early on a June morning to sprinkle the fresh sand. Not the croquet that he played on a summer afternoon, nor the leisurely lawn tennis. Not the young man that he sketched who would be leaning on his croquet mallet asking a question of someone whose muslin dress swept the ground, and who smiled for one brief moment under her sunshade and then turned away. Nor the small boys in sailor suits, nor the little long-haired girls in pinafores, nor the husband and wife reading aloud in turn, upon a winter's evening. Nor the grandmother and the unmarried sister living in the same house, or written to each day and visited; nor the new baby that came every spring. These things were as natural to du Maurier and to his contemporaries as the air they breathed and the ground they walked upon. But with them went deference and courtesy, fidelity and faith, a belief in a man's work and the pride that goes hand in hand with that belief. These fundamental standards wove the pattern of a Victorian day, and the writers and artists of that day became part of the pattern and echoed it in print or upon canvas, stamping it with their individuality, their own genius, creating an era that was at once warm and colourful and prosperous, an age away from our present world of meagre mediocrity.

We who are offered today a so-called wealth of literature from the bookstalls of stations and airports, pulpy pages known as digests or potted shorts, find it hard to understand the part played by *Punch* in the latter half of the nineteenth century. It stood alone, the only weekly paper of its kind. A gibe at the government from *Punch* in 1870, and worried members of Parliament would be discussing the fact in the lobbies the same day. A cool criticism of a picture or a poem, and the luckless author hung his head in shame. Only the best draughtsmen of the day contributed to *Punch*, and with them the wittiest writers, the ablest critics. A successful future was assured to whoever was lucky enough to obtain a permanent place on the *Punch* staff. And George du Maurier was so lucky. When the well-known illustrator Leech died in 1865 he succeeded to his place, although only thirty-one years old. His weekly drawing on the left-hand side, beside the cartoon on the right, soon became the most talked-of page in

Punch, and had he ended his days as a draughtsman only, he would long have been remembered and loved for this work alone.

But in late middle age he wrote two novels, *Peter Ibbetson* and *Trilby*, which somehow found their way into the hearts of his contemporaries in a way few novels have done before or since. The word "hearts" is used intentionally, because the critical mind cannot admit that George du Maurier was a great novelist, in the sense of a Dickens or a Thackeray. As a writer he was careless, and knew little of style or form, and the plots of his novels can be called fantastic, melodramatic, even absurd. Yet these two stories sounded such an echo in the emotions of the men and women of his day, both in this country and throughout the United States of America, that they were read, and reread, and thumbed again, year after year, down to our own time; and not only read, but in some inexplicable fashion deeply loved. When a novel can affect the human heart in such a way it seems to mean one thing only: not that the tale is exceptional in itself, but that the writer has so projected his personality on to the printed page that the reader either identifies with that personality or becomes fascinated by it, and in a sense near hypnotised.

It so happened that the personality of George du Maurier, though never forceful in a strong or domineering way, held great attraction. He radiated a kind of warmth that made people turn to him on sight with sympathy, and as they came to know him better this quality of warmth caught at their hearts, just as his novels caught at his readers'. It is true to say he had no enemies. He was a man well loved. His charm—most wretched word, too often overdone—was never forced, and never insincere. It was a gift from God.

His feeling for family was deep and strong and very French. Not only his affection for his wife and his five children: to him the ties of blood stretched far beyond, to nephews, nieces, cousins and second cousins, so that any who needed help were not afraid to some to him. Ancestors, long buried in French soil and never known, were dear to him; and dearer still the grandchildren and the great-grandchildren he did not live to see.

He was a man of very simple tastes. He loved his home. He had no wish to travel, except to France, or to the Yorkshire fishing port of Whitby, and when his novels made him famous he found himself embarrassed by his fame. "Perhaps Papa will now put electric light in the lumber room," said Gerald, his younger son, when success burst upon his father; but the lumber room remained unlit. George du Maurier saw no reason to change his way of living because he received hundreds of letters every week from perfect strangers. He smiled to himself, and thought it all very peculiar, and went for a long walk on Hampstead Heath: and when he returned he rolled a cigarette and went to his easel in the studio, and continued drawing, or writing, with the continual clatter about him of his family or his friends.

If the fortune he received from *Trilby* remained unspent upon himself, it was because he had the forethought to set it all aside for those who came after him. He remembered his own early days, in Paris and in London, and he saw no reason why his descendants should suffer want if, by the success of his own efforts, he could make provision for them. His own father, Louis-Maturin Busson du Maurier, had not been able to make provision for him, or for his mother, brother and sister, and they had suffered much in consequence. His father had been a delightful, engaging man of many talents, with a beautiful singing voice which his son inherited. Although he was scientist by profession his inventions always failed, in spite of which he lived with unfailing confidence and good humour until the day of his death.

He married Ellen Clarke, the daughter of the notorious

Mary Anne Clarke whose liaison with the Duke of York at the beginning of the century had caused so much scandal. Possibly the memory of those early days had left a permanent strain upon the daughter, because she possessed a more difficult character than her husband Louis-Maturin. She was by nature nervy, anxious and highly strung. Disappointed in the ability of her husband to make a success of life, she concentrated upon her elder son, loving him fiercely and possessively, a love which he returned with real feeling, but fortunately for himself without a sense of strain.

There were three children born of the marriage. George, who was never known as George but always as Kicky, a nickname which he carried to the end of his days, was the eldest, and was born in Paris in 1834. He was brought up there, with his younger brother Eugene, nicknamed Gyggy, and his sister Isobel. His happy childhood and his schooldays he described in *Peter Ibbetson* and in his third, not so successful, novel, *The Martian*.

In spite of his later fame, and his real contentment with his life in Hampstead, he looked back upon those early Paris days with deep nostalgia and almost passionate regret, as though in the depths of him there was a seed of melancholy, a creature unfulfilled, who, longing wistfully for what-was-once and cannot-be-again, comes to the surface with the written word and vanishes, unseen.

That happy childhood was a memory he clung to all his life, all the more so because his adolescence and early manhood were not so blest. The reason for this was that his father, still seeking the fortune that eluded him, left Paris with his family and settled in London, in Pentonville, and for the next few years, until his father died in 1856, young Kicky, to please him, studied chemistry, a subject which he detested and for which he had no aptitude. The younger boy, Gyggy, neglected and misunderstood, had the sense to run away and return to France, where he joined the French army; but his character was lighter and more irresponsible than his brother's and he never had the energy to rise above the rank of corporal, to the shame of his parents and the indifference of himself.

When Louis-Maturin died, Kicky persuaded his mother to let him return to Paris and study art in the studios of the Quartier Latin. He and his brother and sister had drawn brilliantly from an early age, and Kicky felt strongly that unless he could develop this gift freely, without restriction, in the city he loved so well, he would never make anything of his life, but would drift into failure, like his father before him. His mother understood him well enough to know that this was true, so Kicky, her first-born and best-beloved, was given her blessing to follow the career he had chosen for himself.

Back in the Paris he loved, young George du Maurier spent eighteen happy months amongst his fellow students, living the life that Little Billee lived in *Trilby*. His appearance at that time was afterwards described by his great friend Tom Armstrong, in *Reminiscences of du Maurier*. "It is curious," wrote Armstrong, "that my recollection of our first meeting should be so vivid, but I suppose his personality from the beginning attracted me . . . . I can revive the picture of him in my mind's eye sitting astride one of the Utrecht velvet chairs, with his elbows on the back, pale almost to sallowness, square-shouldered and very lean, with no hair on his face except a slight moustache . . . he certainly was very attractive and sympathetic, and the other young fellows with whom I was living felt much as I did. We admired his coats with square shoulders and long skirts after the fashion of the day, and we admired his voice and his singing, his power of drawing portraits and caricatures from memory, his strength and skill with his fists, and above all we were attracted by his very sympathetic manner. I think this certainty of finding sympathy was one of his greatest and most abiding charms. His personality was a very engaging one, and evoked confidence in those who knew him very little. Music was a powerful influence in du Maurier's life. He used to say that literature, painting and sculpture evoked no emotion which could be compared with that felt by a sensitive person on hearing a well-trained voice or a violin . . . in those days he spent much more time at our hired piano than he did before an easel."

The Little Billee existence might have continued much longer, or at least long enough for Kicky to become a great painter, but this was not to be. For suddenly, in the summer of 1858, the tragedy of his life occurred. He lost the sight of his left eye. And for a time it was feared he might lose the sight of both. The agony and misery of the months that followed he described many years later in *The Martian.*

He moved from Antwerp, where he had been sharing a studio with a fellow student, Felix Moschelles, to the little town of Malines. For a while he felt he would never recover from the blow; he even had dark thoughts of suicide. His mother, who came out to be with him, could not comfort him; for though he made light of the tragedy in public, and laughed and joked about it when his friends came to Malines to see him, showing them his dark glasses and saying he was an *aveugle*, she knew, and they suspected, what his inner suffering must be.

Money was scarce. They had nothing to live upon but the annuity his mother had inherited from Mary Anne Clarke, the original hush money from the Duke of York. His brother Gyggy was a constant source of worry, always in debt as his father had been, and his sister Isobel, now a pretty girl of nineteen, must also be supported, for although she played the piano beautifully she could hardly earn her living by doing so, nor was she likely to find herself a rich husband. It seemed to Kicky at that time that he, who had hoped to be the main prop of the family, had become, in a few short months, its greatest liability. It would be better if they were rid of him altogether.

And then Isobel wrote from London, where she was staying with a school friend, Emma Wightwick, to say that Mrs. Wightwick had heard of an oculist at Grafrath, near Düsseldorf, who had cured hundreds of people near to blindness, and who was said in fact to be the finest oculist in Europe. What was more, there was a school for painting in Düsseldorf itself. Why did not Kicky and her mother leave Malines, and try their luck in Germany? This suggestion saved her brother from suicide, and in the spring of 1859 young George du Maurier and his mother moved to Düsseldorf, the charm and gaiety of which went to the young artist's head immediately, and life seemed once more possible.

The oculist could not restore the sight of his left eye, but he did promise that, with care, the right one would remain sound to the end of his days; and so Kicky's natural optimism returned and he began to draw again—he even drew a flattering likeness of the oculist himself—and he and his mother plunged into the lighthearted society of Düsseldorf, where life was bohemian and manners easy, and money did not matter too much because it went so far.

His sister Isobel came out to join them, flirting happily with all the impecunious German counts and princekins, and Kicky did the same with a Miss Lewis, who was the beauty of that particular season. Artist friends drifted down from Paris and Antwerp to join in the fun, and in the work too, which was rather haphazard and not very steady. There were plenty of sketches lying about in the studio which du Maurier shared with a young Swiss friend, all showing promise but few of them finished; and it was not until his closest friend, Tom Armstrong, came to stay in the spring of 1860, and told him frankly that he was doing no good and was allowing himself to drift, that Kicky took stock of himself. Tom was perfectly right. He *was* doing no good. He was living on his mother, he was selling no pictures, and he was getting himself entangled with girls he could not possiby afford to marry.

Tom Armstrong showed him *Punch's Almanack*, which he had brought over from London, and pointed out the drawings of Keene and Leech, insisting that if Kicky chose to do so he could draw as well as either. If a fellow wanted to earn his living by his pencil, London was the place to start, Tom Armstrong urged. He was returning himself in May, he could get Kicky introductions to *Punch* and to other weekly illustrated papers. Several of their friends had moved from Paris to London, and artistic London was a world away from the dreariness of Pentonville and chemical laboratories. There was every reason why the move should be made now, before it was too late and Kicky had allowed himself to settle to the life of a second-rater in a German provincial town. How about it?

Young du Maurier looked about him. The season in Düsseldorf was beginning once again. The same little narrow circles meeting at the same parties. The same concerts, the same idle chatter, the same frothy flirtations meaning nothing. Amusing last year, coming as it did after the anxiety with his eye, but amusing no longer. He was fit again, he was well, and he wanted to draw, he wanted to be independent, and he wanted to be able to keep his mother, instead of his mother keeping him. He was twenty-six. If he did not pull himself together he would become another Gyggy, reduced to the ranks after bad behaviour.

Once again, as in Malines, it was Wightwick influence that finally decided him. Not Mrs. Wightwick this time, but the daughter, Emma. She and her mother had come out to Düsseldorf to see the du Mauriers, and especially

Isobel, who had stayed with them in London. Kicky remembered Emma as a long-legged, handsome schoolgirl, with a plait swinging from her shoulders. She was now grown up and very lovely, with a pair of eyes that made Miss Lewis's seem like boot buttons. When she looked at him, gravely, yet with understanding, it did something to his heart that no woman had done before. He decided to go to London . . . .

So in May 1860, borrowing ten pounds from his mother's annuity, young George du Maurier set forth from Düsseldorf to London, travelling with Tom Armstrong and the Wightwicks. The personality that Tom Armstrong found so sympathetic reveals itself clearly enough in the letters that he wrote to his mother, with the moods at times sanguine, at times despondent, but more often than not eager for life and for experience, and for what he could contribute towards both. In those days he used to feel within himself two persons: the one serious, energetic, full of honest ambition and good purpose; the other a wastrel, reckless and careless, easily driven to the devil. It seemed to him, in such a mood, that only the love and influence of Emma Wightwick could save him from disaster. Possibly, like all young men, he was too introspective. He had yet to learn the philosophy of the middle years. He wrote very fully to his mother, keeping little or nothing from her. He shared with her both his gaiety and his disillusions. Some robust quality of understanding in her, inherited surely from Mary Anne, made it easy for him to be frank with her on matters delicate. She even twitted him, during his long engagement, on his excessive purity, telling him it was bad for his health, and quite unnecessary. Sure of her faith in him, he could not help showing her, from time to time, a little-boy conceit. He was anxious, so desperately anxious, to do well. Therefore he must pretend sometimes that he had already arrived, that editors were running after him, that critics were open-mouthed, that London society—and especially the women of that society—were kneeling at his feet. This quality of cocksureness, this tendency to show off, to talk big, betrayed itself to the mother who bore him as inner doubts and fear of failure, as a sort of bolster to his youthful pride so swiftly wounded by a careless word. Because of it he endeared himself to her all the more, and knowing his faults, unable to help herself, she loved him the better for them.

Emma Wightwick, who was to become his wife, saw no fault in him at all, except that, when he was not with her, he was inclined to become tipsy at evening parties. Also he smoked overmany cigarettes. And sometimes he worked too hard, and stayed up too late, and was apt to talk nonsense to his friends. Besides, rather foolishly, admiring too many pretty faces, which he would sketch from memory on the backs of old envelopes. She felt that Paris had induced bad ways in him which she must correct, and his tendency to think of himself as a Frenchman, and a bohemian, was something it would be better for him to forget. He must learn to become an Englishman, and a respectable one at that. Which indeed he did, without too much agony of the spirit. But that France and its memories still possessed some part of him, he showed in his novels some thirty years later . . .

There is a description of him by a contemporary, the daughter of Frith the artist, who, writing her memoirs in 1908, remembered young George du Maurier in the 1860s, when he had not been married very long, and was still making his way in the London world. Here is what she says of him:

"When I first knew du Maurier he was living in rooms over a shop quite close to the British Museum, and in great terror of losing his sight.

"He was never a robust man, but had immense vitality,

and was one of those charming natures which give out hope, life, and amusement to all who come in contact with them, and I should sum him up in one word—joyous. Naturally he had his dark days and times, but these he never showed in public. In the days I knew him he was not at all well off, and he had an increasing family, but he had married one of those wives of that period, the women who lived for their homes and their husbands, and there was not a load that Mrs. du Maurier did not take from his shoulders when she could, not a thing she would not do to help him, and see that no small worries stood between him and his work.

"She was one of the loveliest creatures of her time, and from her statuesque beauty her husband drew his inspiration, and has immortalised her over and over again in the pictures in *Punch*. She had quantities of lovely dark hair, and in those days often twisted a yellow riband among her locks with a most ravishing effect. It was always a delight to me to watch du Maurier draw, while Mrs. du Maurier sat and sewed, and the children played about the floor unchecked.

"Du Maurier became a rich man, and had a big house, but I question if any days were happier, although all were happy, than those first days when he sang at his work in the front room over the corner shop . . . .

"His talk was most delightful, but above all the delight caused me by his singing is a thing I shall never forget.

"He woud sit down to the piano, and in a moment the room would be full of divine melody, not loud, not declamatory, but music in the fullest sense of the word; a nightingale singing in an orchard full of apple blossom was not as sweet, and I have heard a sudden hush come over a large assembly should he sing, albeit he liked a small audience. I have only to close my eyes, and I can hear him once more—a perfect silence would fall upon us all.

"*Der Lieben Langen Tag* wailed out across the night, and I was gazing at the moon across the sea, listening to the mingled ripple of the waves on the shore and the lovely voice in the drawing-room, my eyes filling with tears, I do not quite know why, and my heart beating as sentimentally as that of any lovesick maiden in her 'teens. Never did any moon shine before or since as that did, or any sea and voice mingle as did those. Then the tone would change; dainty little ripples ran along the keys of the piano; we were in France. Despite the very obvious moonlight on the sea the sun shone, soldiers clanked along the boulevard, girls came out and beckoned and smiled, the leaves rustled on the trees, and all was spring, and gaiety and pleasure. One never had to ask him to continue; one little song after another would make the evening memorable; he knew his audience, knew that we could never have enough, and he played upon us all with his voice, another Orpheus with his lute, until we travelled miles into the country of make-believe, and wandered with him along the myriad roads of fancy. How wish could reproduce that *voix d'or*! At any rate, I possess it always, and can never forget the evenings when we were sung to by du Maurier.

"I always think that those who knew and loved such a genius as his can never lose him; he may die, he himself may pass into the shadows, but how much he leaves behind...."

THE MATINEE IDOL

[1973]

My father Gerald was born on the twenty-sixth of March 1873, so if he were alive today he would be a hundred years old. The words make no sense to me, and by no possible feat of the imagination can I conjure up a vision of some lean and slippered pantaloon sitting in a wheelchair, propped up by pillows, deaf, perhaps, mouth half open, fumbling for telegrams of congratulation.

When he died on April 11, 1934, at the comparatively early age of sixty-one, after an operation for cancer—and I have it on good authority that with the surgical skill and medical treatment of today they could have saved him— he knew, despite plans for convalescence and smiles of re- assurance to my mother, sitting by his bedside (he died on the thirty-first anniversary of their wedding day), that his time had come. Ripe old age was not for him. The weeks and months ahead held no promise. He had neither the energy nor the inclination to read plays which he would be bored to direct and equally bored to perform; and as for hanging about a film studio all day waiting to speak half a dozen lines that would later be cut, this might serve to pay off what he owed for income tax, but would only increase the sense of apathy within. To what end? An expression he often used in those last years, half joking, half serious, and then would follow it up with his favourite quotation: "Now more than ever seems it rich to die, to cease upon the midnight with no pain."

Well, he had his wish. He had no pain. My aunt, who was with him at the time, told me he had a curious, puzzled look in his eyes, as if asking a question. I can believe it. He had the same look when I smiled at him from the doorway and waved good-bye before his operation.

This is no way to start an article about a matinee idol. The end before the beginning. The trouble is that, as his daughter, I never saw the beginning, only grew up through childhood and adolescence when the tide of his popularity was running at full flood. He was thirty-three in 1906, a year before I was born, when he made his first big success as Raffles, the cricketer turned cracksman, a play packed full of action from start to finish, a novelty in those days, which delighted his Edwardian audiences as much as a similar theme about a Georgie Best turning out to be one of the Great Train Robbers would enthrall a pack of shouting teen-age fans in 1973. In 1906, however, his applauders were not children—except on half holidays: they were respectable fathers of families, middle-aged matrons, wide-eyed spinsters, stolid businessmen, sisters and aunts up from the country, anyone and everyone who had money enough in his pocket to pay for a seat in gallery, pit or stall, and desired above all things not to be made to think but to be entertained. It was exciting, and rather shocking, to have the hero of a play a burglar—and not an obvious burglar, the spinster ladies told themselves, who wore a cloth cap and a muffler, but a gentleman strolling about with his hands in his pockets. It gave them a *frisson*. And the men in the audience nodded in agreement. Nonsense, of course, but jolly good fun, and how easy du Maurier made the whole thing look, from lighting a cigarette to handling a gun. No wonder the women were mad about him.

Easy, perhaps, but in 1906 this sort of acting was new, and a critic of the day was even more impressed than the audience. "To play such a scene as this, slowly but surely working to a tremendous emotional climax, with few words and the difficulty of an assumed calmness which needs much subtlety, is the achievement of a tragedian of uncommon quality."

I wonder if Gerald read this notice and whether, for a moment, he thought, "Tragedian? Me? Could I ever? Dare I ever?" then, with a smile, threw the thought away with the newspaper, and continued to give his public what it wanted. Arsène Lupin, a French crook and a duke, Jimmy Valentine, the safe opener, one impossible con man after another, and the greatest crook of them all Hubert Ware in George Bancroft's *The Ware Case*, who murdered his brother-in-law by drowning him in a lake, and lied his way out of the witness box with the help of a down-at-heel accomplice. Immoral, if you come to think of it. No message to the masses. It did not send the audiences home pondering about world problems (it was first produced in 1915, and the men who shouted their applause were all in khaki), but it allowed them to forget that they were going back to the trenches: the murder of a brother-in-law in a lake made sense and war did not.

Lists of plays that were popular successes between the years 1906 and 1918, all produced at Wyndham's Theatre, where Gerald had gone into management in 1910 with a non-acting partner, Frank Curzon, would be of little interest to the reader of 1973. He will never see them. None, except those of J. M. Barrie, is likely to be revived. Suffice it to say they were of their era, and Gerald, who had a genius for knowing when the moment was ripe for something old or something new, a revival once popular and acclaimed a second time or a novelty catching the passing mood, never failed to "bring them in," as the saying went. "House Full" boards went up outside the theatre, the queues lengthened, the taxis rolled.

This, it could be argued by the young of today, sounds somewhat tame. Bourgeois, middle class. Nothing like a

Pop Festival in Hyde Park or the Isle of Wight, where boys and girls will sleep out in the open and wait twenty-four hours in the rain to hear the beloved reach for his mike or twang his guitar. Football players are mobbed as they leave the ground, film stars (and they grow fewer every day) beseiged outside their hotels, disc jockeys accosted in the streets; anyone who happens to hit the headlines in the morning appears on television that same evening and is seen by millions. Instant fame is the order of the day. Herein lies the difference between our time and forty, fifty, sixty years ago. There was no hysteria then. Applause, yes, and plenty of it, and boos and catcalls too, when a play had offended, reviews the following morning written by critics of repute who did not hesitate to damn author and cast alike if they deserved it, yet at the same time spared the newspaper reader the cheap gibe or flourish of wit.

Dignity, perhaps, was the operative word. Dignity, and ease of manner. Recognition of talent, technique and training, and understanding on the part of critic and play-goer alike that the men and women on the other side of the footlights had worked long and hard during the weeks of rehearsal to bring pleasure to those who sat and watched. If they had failed, too bad; the play would be withdrawn, the cast dismissed, the management lose money, and a start must begin all over again to find a play that would please the audience better.

A point in favour of the old actor-manager of the past was that those he endeavoured to entertain connected him with one particular theatre. The playgoers from 1910 to 1925 did not have to search the newspapers to discover where Gerald du Maurier was performing: it could only be at Wyndham's Theatre. (And after 1924, when the partnership with Frank Curzon ended and Gilbert Miller took his place, the St. James's Theatre became the new home.) The cast changed, of course, from play to play, but there was continuity in the theatre staff, the commissionaire in front of the theatre, the stage doorkeeper, the cleaners, the dressers, the stage manager, the manager in the box office. Thinking back, after all too many years, I can feel the swings doors with the bars across them under my hands; surely I had to reach up to them? And Bob, the stage door-keeper, smiling down from his stool. The stairs to the dressing room, stage entrance on the left, stairs to the other dressing rooms on the right. The musty, indefinable theatre smell of shifting scenery, with stage hands moving about and Poole, Gerald's dresser, who had rather a red face and mumbled as he spoke, hovering at the entrance to the dressing room.

The colour of the room, in retrospect, seems to be green. There were playbills all over the wall on the left. A large mirror on the right, and a flat sort of divan beneath it on which my sisters and I used to sit. It was good for dangling our legs. A curtain, seldom pulled, divided the inner sanctum where Gerald changed and made up. A different smell came from it, not musty—grease paint (I'm told they don't use it today), eau de cologne and some-thing else, cool, clean, that must have been Gerald himself.

To us children there was nothing singular or surprising that in a moment he would come bursting in from the door that led direct to backstage, calling for Poole, and that we would hear the distant sound of applause which meant that the audience was still clapping after the final curtain, be-fore "God Save the King." This was his life. Other children's fathers, perhaps, went to an office; ours went to the theatre. Then, maybe, friends or acquaintances who had been to the matinee would come round to see him, which meant standing up and shaking hands on our part, and listening, yawning, while the chatter passed over our heads. The people who came always seemed excited, thrill-ed, entering the star's dressing room was an event. It was a relief when the exclamations and the congratulations were over and we were just ourselves, with Gerald sitting down and taking off his makeup at the dressing table. Pity, though, I sometimes thought. He looked nicer with it on, bolder, somehow, and his eyes very bright. Still, it was all part of the game of make-believe that was his, and ours as well. Life was pretending to be someone else. Otherwise it was rather dull.

I suppose I must have been about six, or possibly seven, when I first realised that Gerald—Daddy, as we called him—was recognised, known, by strangers outside the theatre. We were entering a restaurant—it was probably the Piccadilly Hotel, because he had not yet started his custom of going to the Savoy, and for some reason or other he was taking us out to lunch; perhaps it was my elder sister Angela's birthday. There were several people standing about and I was lagging behind. Then a tall woman— all adults seem unbearably tall to a small child—nudged her companion with a knowing look and said, "There's Gerald du Maurier." She sounded excited, and there was a gleam in her eye. The escort turned and stared, and a knowing look came into his eye too. Both of them smirked. Somehow, I don't know why, I found this offensive. I looked up sharply at my father, but he was humming softly under his breath, as he often did, and took not the slightest notice of either the tall woman or her escort, but I knew that he had heard the exclamation, and he knew that I had heard it too. Waiters suddenly approached, bowing, pulling back chairs from our table. Heads turned. The same gleam, the same nudge. We sat down and the business of the lunch proceeded, and the whole scene sank into a child's unconscious mind, but the penny had dropped.

From then on I knew that strangers, people we should never speak to, were in some curious way gratified when he passed by. The applause, the clapping of hands, the little knot of men and women, mostly women, waiting outside the stage door when we left the theatre to go home after a

matinee, was all part of the same thing. Because Gerald—
Daddy—had pleased them by pretending to be someone
else, like Raffles leaping out of the grandfather clock in
that last act, he also pleased them by going into a restaurant and having lunch. And the strange thing was that
it made *them* feel important, not him. He didn't care. And
somehow, to a child of six or seven, this was tremendously
important. If Gerald had smirked back, or thrown them a
glance over his shoulder—those two in the restaurant—or
in any way shown himself aware . . . *my* idol would have
crashed.

This cool disregard on the part of the well-known towards the pointer, the starer, was not, I think, peculiar to
Gerald, but was characteristic of his fellow stars as well,
half a century and more ago. They were not concerned
about their image. I suspect that it is different today. With
rare exceptions a public figure who does not wave, grin,
exchange jokes with his admirers and continually show
himself conscious of his fans would be accused of having
a swollen head. The fact that Gerald ignored nudges and
whispers in the street or in restaurants did not mean that
he despised the crowds who came to applaud him in the
theatre, or indeed the many fans who wrote to him or
waited outside the stage door, autograph book in hand.
Letters were answered promptly, though I have no recollection of who did the secretarial work before my aunt
Sybil—Billy, my mother's sister—took it on around 1919.
Hands were shaken, autographs written, and all with a
good grace, after the matinee, in that dark passage between Wyndham's and what was then the New Theatre;
then to the car drawn up at the front of the house, with
Dan—or was it Martin?—throwing open the door, and so
back home for an early dinner at a quarter to seven, then
twenty minutes' shut-eye before the evening performance.
Eight performances a week, bed never before midnight or
later, but first supper—eggs and bacon or sausages—cook-

ed by my mother, who had waited up for him in her dressing gown and now listened to the gossip of his day.

Stage, film and T.V. stars nowadays have marriages that come apart with the first row. An absence for a few weeks on tour or on location is asking for trouble. Somebody's eye wanders, is caught, and the curious modern custom of telling all to the innocent partner so as to appease personal guilt is followed through to its inevitable conclusion, and the innocent partner, pride outraged, sues for a divorce. Everyone marries again. Perhaps it will be second or third time lucky.

Gerald, who had learnt the facts of life as a young actor from Mrs. Patrick Campbell and others, fell in love with my mother, Muriel Beaumont, when they were acting together in Barrie's *The Admirable Crichton* at the Duke of York's Theatre in 1902. She was very pretty, rather naïve, had a will of her own and adored him. Adoration was mutual, and continued unchanging until his death thirty-one years after their marriage in 1903. How fully my mother was aware of his wandering eye I shall never know. Perhaps she closed her own, realising, with the wisdom of her particular generation, that he would always place her first. Not a marriage of convenience, but a marriage of love and understanding. Twice I saw her really roused, with a high colour and stamping foot. The first occasion was when she opened her bill from Fortnum & Mason and saw, in the middle of a list of items she had ordered, a large case of tea that had been sent round, on Gerald's instructions, to the apartment of his current leading lady. Let him order goods on the side if he must, she told him, but not put them down to his wife.

The second occasion was more serious. Driving into London from Hampstead in her own small car, she noticed, with astonishment, Gerald's Sunbeam parked outside a terrace house on the fringe of St. John's Wood. The house was inhabited by a young actress who had a small part in his current production. My mother—Mo, as she was always called—drove on to town, whether to shop or to visit friends I don't know, but on the return journey, a few hours later, she saw that the Sunbeam was still there. Crisis threatened. Dinner before the theatre that evening was an ordeal. I know, because I was there. What passed between my father and my mother in the way of accusation, denial, acknowledgement, contrition, I shall never know, except for the quick whisper in my ear from Gerald on his way to the theatre, "Mummy's so angry with me, I don't know what to do." How old was I? Nineteen, twenty? I don't remember; but I felt then as if he were my brother, or indeed my son. The father-daughter relationship had entered a deeper phase.

Ten years or so previously the relationship had been more personal, more emotional. If Gerald's most popular successes to date—and I am now speaking of 1917—had been chiefly those of what we should now call the cops and robbers variety, the thrill of the chase, it took J. M. Barrie to draw the finest acting out of the matinee idol of the day. In *Dear Brutus*, surely Barrie's best play, the least sentimental, the most perceptive, Gerald took the part of a jaded, spoilt successful painter, at odds with his wife and with the world. The title—taken from Cassius in *Julius Caesar*, "The fault, dear Brutus, is not in our stars, But in ourselves, that we are underlings"—gives the theme of the play: a group of people, the painter amongst them, as they wander in an enchanted wood, are shown, by their host magician, what they would have done with their lives had they been given a second chance. Gerald, as Will Dearth, is still an artist, but unsuccessful, with no possessions except a daughter in her teens, whom he loves, and who loves him. The transformation of the jaded, successful man in the first act to the happy-go-lucky father in the second saw Gerald at his peak. He was himself, yes, but also every man who carries in his soul a seed of discontent, of wishing that his world was other than it had turned out to be. There was nostalgia, too—memories of his own artist father, who had known success but had remained his generous, unspoilt self.

The third act brought realisation. The second chance was nothing but a dream. He was Will Dearth, who had conquered the artistic world, but he had no daughter. "When I was in the wood with Margaret," Gerald said, "she . . . she . . . Margaret . . ." and then he lifted his head and looked about him, at the walls of the house enclosing him, no wood, no child, and it was as though he shrank into himself, and the expression in his eyes, bewildered, lost, anguished, was something that his real daughter, a child of ten, has never forgotten, can never forget. Filial identification? Possibly. But the hushed audience identified also, and this is surely the whole meaning of communication between the actor on the stage and those who sit and watch him; they have a bond in common, they see themselves.

The natural school of acting that Gerald founded had much to answer for in later years. Mumbled speaking, sloppy gestures, actors with small talent believing that, without years of training and hard thought, they could walk an easy road to success. It was not so. Either they achieved a temporary popularity, or they fell by the way. Only those with real genius knew how to develop the technique and build upon it, and I do not think it is fancy on my part, or filial pride, when I think of the two greatest actors of our day, Laurence Olivier and John Gielgud, who, in their youth, must have seen *Dear Brutus* and watched Gerald in his prime.

It can be argued, of course, that when Gerald appeared on the stage for the first time in 1894, at the age of twenty-one, without any training, he did so through favouritism. Sir John Hare happened to be a friend of his father and was pleased to give the lad the humble part of Fritz the

waiter, with little to do and still less to say. His only experience until then had been in amateur theatricals during
school holidays from Harrow, and at Harrow his sole
claim to distinction had been his ability to imitate Sir
Henry Irving up and down the corridors, to the amusement of masters and boys alike. Possibly an added induce-
ment to Sir John Hare was the fact that two years
previously the boy's father, George du Maurier, had published his novel *Trilby*, which had proved to be the literary
event of the season in both England and America. The
Punch artist, a celebrity anyway, was now world famous.
Nothing succeeds like success, and it is doubtful if the
critic who wrote of Fritz the waiter, "Mr. du Maurier in
a very few words showed that he had probably found his
vocation" would have noticed the young man but for the
familiar name in the programme.

A familiar name on its own, however, does not carry its
bearer far unless the talent is there, and the will to work,
and Gerald possessed not only talent but determination
too, qualities that were developed in the following years
under the brilliant tuition of Beerbohm Tree and Mrs.
Patrick Campbell. From Fritz the waiter to Will Dearth
may not have been a hard road or an uphill climb, but it
took three-and-twenty years to achieve, which is a fair step,
if you come to think of it. Charm and ease of manner may
win popularity in a night, but artistic genius within a man
must be nurtured by perception, experience and integrity,
if it is to survive for more than a decade.

"Why was Daddy knighted?" I asked my mother when,
after his death in 1934, I was making notes for his bio-
graphy. She looked up from her embroidery with a
thoughtful expression in her eyes. "I don't think we ever
knew," she replied, which seemed to me then, and now, a
delightful attitude to honours, and one that was undoubtedly Gerald's own. I assumed that the knighthood
was laid upon him in 1922 not because of the wild popu-

larity of Bulldog Drummond, a very different role from that of Will Dearth, nor for the somewhat quixotic gesture which he made in his mid-forties in 1918 by throwing up *Dear Brutus* and joining the Irish Guards as a cadet (a tribute, I suspect, to his beloved brother Guy, who had been killed in action in 1915), but plainly and simply "for services rendered to his profession." He was president not only of the Actors' Orphanage but of a number of other charitable organisations, never sparing himself when he could make money for those less fortunate than himself. Wasn't it Will Dearth in the enchanted wood who had said to his daughter Margaret, "We lucky ones, let's always be kind to those who are down on their luck, and when we're kind, let's be a little kinder"? No one ever asked Gerald for a loan and was refused, and needless to say the money, if any attempt was made to return it, was not accepted. He was never a rich man, as riches are known today in the world of film and pop star, but what he earned was generously spent, needy relatives taken care of, friends paid for on holiday. Make other people happy while you have the means to do so, and to hell with the future and the Inland Revenue . . . .

If the matinee idol of the war years was now Sir Gerald with added responsibilities, he carried the burden lightly; and although in the 1920s he was the undoubted head of his profession, and had turned fifty, he was still youthful in appearance and young in heart. No one who remembers *The Last of Mrs Cheyney*—Freddie Lonsdale's witty comedy at the St. James's Theatre—in which he co-starred with Gladys Cooper, will forget the brilliance of these two, their consummate ease and grace, their timing, the sense of fun that pervaded the whole production. Now there were two set of fans waiting at the stage door after a performance. His and hers. And if nobody screamed or fainted when Gladys finally emerged, I do recollect the murmur that arose from her excited adorers, gradually swelling in volume as she passed between them, and hands would be stretched out to touch her coat as though the very texture had magic properties. Gladys smiled, and waved, and made a dash for her car, and if by chance I scrambled in her wake, being an adorer in my own fashion, I used to wonder how swiftly a waiting crowd might be moved to anger, the murmur of approval turn to a roar of hate, the hands outstretched to reach down for stones. Anyone who has heard boos and groans and whistles at a first night after a flop will understand me.

The great day for the fans, of course, was the annual Theatrical Garden Party, in aid of the Actors' Orphanage, originally held in the Botanical Garden in Regent's Park, but in postwar years in the Chelsea Hospital Gardens. This would be the nearest thing, fifty years ago, to the pop festivals of our own time. The whole theatrical profession would be there, stars, supporting players, understudies. The sight was something between a circus and a fun fair. Walk up . . . walk up . . . Come bowl for a pig with Owen Nares. Dig for buried treasure with Phyllis Dare. Buy Gladys Cooper Face Cream from her own hands. The biggest draw, as might be expected, was a vast marquee at the end of the grounds covering a built-up stage, with a curtain and rows of seats for a paying audience, where Gerald, with a picked cast of actors and actresses, gave a knockabout performance known as *The Grand Giggle*. If memory serves me right, the skit or farce would last about thirty minutes, the action proceeding at a cracking pace to whoops of laughter. Then the audience would troop out to allow their successors in the queue outside to take their place. An exhausting afternoon for the players, but a field day for the fans. Even the performers' families basked in reflected glory. My mother, with a bevy of helpers, would preside over a hoopla stall with all the grace of a queen consort, with my sisters and myself as a doubtful added attraction, the whispered "Ooh! aren't they dears?" bringing blushes to our cheeks. It was much more fun to roam the other stalls incognito than to pose as prize exhibits.

Well, it's all over now. Grand Giggles and hoopla stalls belong to a bygone age. Some of those who drew the crowds in the twenties now live in the Denville Home for retired actors and actresses, of which Gerald was also president. The art of acting is ephemeral, especially in the theatre. We can see the film stars of yesterday in yesterday's films, hear the voices of poets and singers on a record, keep the plays of dead dramatists upon our bookshelves, but the actor who holds his audience captive for one brief moment upon a lighted stage vanishes forever when the curtain falls. The actors and actresses of two generations ago live on in the memories of those who had the good fortune to watch them and applaud, and if this is poor consolation for the absence of voice and smile and gesture, at least something of their presence lingers still, to bring courage and inspiration to their successors.

When a young player today glances instinctively over his shoulder, alters position, changes tone and speaks with greater clarity—none of which has been laid down for him in the script or urged upon him by the director—is it fanciful to believe that something of the talent possessed by others has brushed off on his shoulders, and that as he treads the boards of a well-worn stage the very dust of a predecessor rises to become part of him? Sentimental, perhaps, but your born actor has sentiment bred in the bone, and superstition too. He feels, he is aware, and no matter how many theatres fall on the scrap heap—the St. James's is no more, the old Criterion is threatened, Wyndham's may one day give place to an office block—the few square acres of London where he works, from Covent Garden to Piccadilly and beyond, are haunted by a happy breed of men who one and all were strolling players in their time. Applause was theirs for a night and a day in their world of make-believe, but the emotion they engendered in themselves and in those about them was for posterity.

When I think of Gerald—and scarcely a day passes without some reminder, from the photographs and mementoes round the house down to his signet ring, which I wear upon my finger—it is not as a father that I see him most clearly, bowling to us children at cricket on the lawn at Hampstead and assuming a different personality with each delivery of the ball; nor as the producer, directing rehersals of a play with intense concentration from a corner of the stage or from the stalls; nor yet as the actor, putting every ounce of energy and thought into a first-night performance and then standing, with the cast beside him, to take his bow and receive the shouting acclaim at the final curtain. No, he has pottered downstairs to the drawing room one fine morning in search of cigarettes, while Mo is upstairs having a bath, and he is wearing silk pyjamas from Beale & Inman of Bond Street, topped by a very old cardigan full of holes that once belonged to his mother. He switches on the gramophone, and the hit song of the day, a sensuous waltz, floats upon the air. He holds out his arms to a nonexistent partner and, closing his eyes, circles the room with the exaggerated rhythm of a musical-comedy hero, languid, romantic, murmuring with mock passion:

> "I wonder why you keep me waiting,
> Charmaine, my Charmaine . . ."

Unseen by friends or fans, and unobserved, so he imagines, by any member of his family, Gerald obeys the instinct of a lifetime, and is acting to himself.

SYLVIA'S BOYS

All childhood memories are visual. A face, a figure, some-body smiling or frowning, and the image stays forever. A moment in time, held captive. Sometimes the drone of adult conversation sounding as a foreign language sud-denly becomes clear. A sentence becomes imprinted on the memory box. No explanation. Silence again.

I do not remember my aunt Sylvia, the second daughter of my grandfather George du Maurier, and the little I do know was told to me, through the years, by my father Gerald, the youngest of the family. He adored all three sisters, and his brother, but somehow I formed the impres-sion that Sylvia, who married Arthur Llewelyn-Davies and bore him five sons, was the sister he loved the best. As I have said, I do not remember her, for she died when I was barely three years old; yet my mother used to tell me that she would ask for me to be taken down to see her, when she was lying in bed already suffering from the cancer that would kill her, so that she could hold me in her arms. This was no mark of favouritism. My sister Angela would go too. But Sylvia adored babies. So I have often wondered why my memory box does not hold the impression of that dying woman, beautiful, witty, tender and loving, whis-pering words of comfort, or possibly even jokes, to a shy and stubborn baby.

I am three, I am four, I am five, and why is it that Cousin Jack, Aunt Sylvia's second son, already a midshipman surely in naval uniform, takes to calling at Cumberland Terrace, where we live, to bring me sweets, and once a balloon?

"Someone to see you," says the parlourmaid. "Just go into the dining room."

I wander in and he is there, sitting in the chair at the far end of the room.

"Hullo, Daphne," and he stands up and smiles at me. At four, at five years old, I am smitten on the spot. Cousin Jack is the only one in the world for me. But now, in retrospect, why did he come? Was it because he knew that his mother Sylvia loved little children, and when I sat on her bed as a baby he remembered this? I do not know.

The image of Cousin Jack persists. He has come to see all of us in the country, where we are spending the summer. He climbs an enormous tree in the garden with supreme confidence. Yet to enter the dining room and say, "Hullo, Cousin Jack," overwhelms me with shyness. My heart beats. I nearly faint with embarrassment.

Another image. We are at Ramsgate. Our grandmother takes a house there every summer. We go to stay, and the cousins too. I overhear my mother say, "I don't know why the Davies boys have to have the best front rooms, and our children are put at the back."

At five, six, I know the answer. The Davies boys are *boys*. Hurrah for them! They are all playing in a front room, and we join them. Some sort of hide-and-seek, and Cousin Michael knocks into me inadvertently. I begin to cry. Cousin Michael rushes from the room. Cousin Nico, nearer to my age, though some four years older, comforts me.

"Look. Look at this picture in *Punch* of a plum pudding. It's Michael."

This is funny. I stop crying and laugh.

"Come and see Michael, he's ashamed," says Nico. We go into the adjoining room. Michael is sitting in a chair with a rug over his face. "Kiss him," says Nico, "go on." Instinctively I know that, although I would like to kiss Cousin Michael, he would not want me to do so.

Overheard conversation. It is between their nanny, Mary, and ours.

"Michael has bad nightmares. He dreams of ghosts coming through the window." Yes . . . Yes . . . I stare at the window of our night nursery in London, and I understand. But what about Peter Pan? Peter Pan came through the window to the night nursery of the Darling children, and he was not a ghost. *Peter Pan.* The play that we act in our own nursery endlessly. The play that we go to see every Christmas. Uncle Jim, who wrote the play for the cousins, and looks after them now that Uncle Arthur and Aunt Sylvia are dead, comes to see us act it in our nursery. But I don't remember when he came.

The memory box switches to Cousin George, the eldest of our cousins; he is tall and dark, smiling down at us from another seaside house at Bournemouth that our grandmother rented. Almost a man. Not a boy.

"Let's all play hide-and-seek in the garden," somebody says—Nico? It will be doubly exciting if Cousin George will play too.

"Doris will play as well," say Nico, always game for anything.

Cousin George looks embarrassed. "I don't think I'll play," he says. "You children go instead."

Am I seven years old? I can't remember. But the thought came to me then, "Perhaps Cousin George would feel shy if he caught Doris." Doris is our nursemaid.

And almost instantly it's the war. Uncle Guy, Daddy's brother, is killed. And a few weeks later we are told, back in Cumberland Terrace, that Cousin George has been killed like Uncle Guy. We wear black bands on our arms for both of them. And the following Sunday we are at the zoo. Uncle Jim is there, with Nico, and we stare at the lion's cage. But surely if Cousin George has been killed we should not go to the zoo? I don't understand. I am confused. Why aren't Uncle Jim and Nico crying? Nico is laughing at the lions. Daddy cried when Uncle Guy was killed. Angela, Jeanne and I have no brother. Why? I shall pretend to be a boy, then. Like the lady who acts Peter Pan at the Duke of York's.

Three years pass. They are rehearsing *Dear Brutus* at Wyndham's Theatre. Uncle Jim and J. M. Barrie merge into one person, and I am no longer a child. I understand what is happening. Daddy—Gerald—has to be the father of a girl called Margaret, and they are alone together in a magic wood. I began to identify. The daughter might be me. Then Uncle Jim calls me up on to the stage.

"Daphne? Shall we show Faith Celli how to walk?"

Up and down, up and down, he takes my hand and we walk together. Everyone rehearsing watches. But I can't identify any more. I feel silly, awkward. Daddy tells me to go back again and watch the rehearsal from the stalls. I know then I would hate to be an actress. I couldn't even be Peter Pan.

Meanwhile the cousins have grown up. Jack, the one-time idol, is married, out of my thoughts. Peter, a more distant figure, also a grown man. Michael, whom I wanted to kiss and never did, is at Oxford. Nico is at Eton, and sometimes we go to the great day there, the Fourth of June, and although he is still the same laughing, joking Nico there is a grandeur about him, he is in Pop, he belongs to the élite.

I am fourteen, no longer a child, at any rate in my own eyes, and one day, saying the customary "Good morning" to our parents in the bedroom, I hear the dreadful news. The night before Uncle Jim had gone round to Wyndham's Theatre and said to our father Gerald, "Michael's dead . . . Drowned." And he broke down, there, in the dressing room. I can't put it out of my mind. Uncle Jim loved Michael best of all the boys. There is a funeral. Michael is

83

buried in Aunt Sylvia's grave, next to Grandpapa and Granny, in the Hampstead churchyard. Michael, I never knew you as we all know Nico, where have you gone? Why did it happen?

One morning, some days after the funeral, when we go for our daily walk into the town to buy biscuits or whatever is needed in our schoolroom, I slip away from the governess and buy some violets with my pocket money. Then I go to the churchyard and put them on the grave. "These are for you, Michael." Perhaps he heard. But would he be there? I don't know. Then I go quickly away to find the others. "Where *have* you been?" No answer. I shan't tell anyone. Let them scold. Aunt Sylvia, George, Michael, perhaps they are all laughing at me together.

The years pass. Ten, twenty, thirty years, the remaining boys are married, myself as well, and I am now a writer, Peter and Nico publishers. Uncle Jim is dead. Peter wants to bring out a book about our grandfather, George du Maurier, and asks me to write the Introduction. Peter, the shadowy boyhood figure, becomes a close friend. We meet at the Café Royal, and talk and talk. Always about family; ours. Grandfather George is Kicky to us, as he was to himself and to his friends. We never discuss the world of today. Always the past. Do all of us carry a seed of melancholy within, except perhaps Nico? Peter thought yes, I could not be sure. Then, within a few years, Peter himself was dead. Jack was dead. Nico, dear Nico, remains.

MY NAME IN LIGHTS

[1958]

I believe that success and the enjoyment of it are a very
personal and a very private thing, like saying one's prayers
or making love. The outward trappings are embarrassing,
and spoil achievement. There come moments in the life of
every artist, whether he be a writer, actor, painter, com-
poser, when he stands back, detached, and looks at what
he has done a split second, perhaps, after he has done it.
That is the supreme moment. It cannot be repeated. The
last sentence of a chapter, the final brush stroke, a bar in
music, a look in the eye and the inflection of an actor's
voice, these are the things that well up from within and
turn the craftsman into an artist, so that, alone in his
study, in his studio, on the stage (and the stage behind the
footlights can be the loneliest place on earth), he has this
blessed spark of intuition. "This is good. This is what I
meant."

The feeling has gone in the next breath, and the craftsman takes over again. Back to routine, and the job for
which he is trained. The pages that must link the story together, dull but necessary; the background behind the
sitter's head; the scenes in the actor's part which come of
necessity as anticlimax: all these are measures of discipline
the artist puts upon himself and understands, and he works
at them day after day, week after week. The moment of
triumph is a thing apart. It is the secret nourishment. The
raison d'être.

The moment, rare and precious, must never be confused with those occasions which come, alas, only too often, when the writer—full of complaisance and conceit—becomes blunted to his own style, and believes he has only to dash off a few thousand words and the result is literature. The moment of the inner glow, and the purr of pleasure, are two very opposite things. The inner glow can bring despair in its train, or a high temperature, or such fever of intensity that nothing but a ten-mile walk or an icy swim will break the spell and release the writer to the world of day-by-day. The purr of pleasure is an indication that the writer has never left the world at all. He has been watching himself at work, hearing his own voice; and the fret with which he waits for public opinion—the criticism of friend, publisher, reader—points to the doubt within. He must be praised, he must be flattered, he must be boosted by some means other than his own life spark: otherwise there is no momentum, all is sound and fury, signifying nothing.

The supreme moment can come to anyone, from Shakespeare penning a sonnet to a clown turning a double somersault. The flash is no respecter of persons, but each and all share one thing in common at the moment of impact, and that is integrity. A kind of purity within. Like a prayer, like the giving of love to a beloved, the feeling says, "This is what I have to offer." Anatole France put it best when he wrote his story of the Juggler of Notre Dame, who, demanding no audience, his being filled with the inner glow, did his circus turn before the statue of the Blessed Virgin, a tribute and a triumph all in one.

After the private homage the public homage is anticlimax, and worse than anticlimax, second rate. Values go awry. We have learnt in our generation to misdoubt, even to dread, mass hysteria. The mob which sobs and screams at a boy with a guitar is the same mob which hanged

Mussolini and his mistress upside down. Tip the scales, and the hands that acclaim the artist become the hands that tear him to pieces. The wreath of laurel is the crown of thorns. The actor and the writer are especially vulnerable today, when world-wide publicity through press and television makes them into that treacherous thing, a "personality."

In other days rogues, vagabonds and scribblers clung together, if they clung at all, and, gently mocked at as a race apart, were left mercifully alone. In the 1950s they are expected to pronounce on the H-bomb, enter Parliament, open hospitals, shut bazaars, and—surely the most surprising activity of the lot—crown carnival queens! In moments of cynicism I like to ponder on what would have happened over a hundred years ago if two sisters from Haworth had been inveigled into Leeds for an afternoon at an art gallery, and found themselves thrust upon a stage before a gaping audience while ringing tones announced, "Charlotte and Emily Brontë, This Is Your Life . . ."

Certainly no moment of triumph for them. Only disgust and horror. Living as we do in an age of noise and bluster, success is now measured accordingly. We must all be seen, and heard, and on the air. What toothpaste do we use? Do our husbands snore? What about A.I.D. and foot and mouth? To answer these questions counts as sucking up. To refuse to answer is high-hat. No remedy for the artist today.

My own dislikes of the trappings of success dates from watching my father, the theatre idol of his time, push his way through a crowd after a first night. Adoring, and fiercely proud, I felt instinctively as a small child that the clamour was false, the praise unreal. What the mob really wants is for the artist to fail, so that the whispering campaign can begin. "Poor chap, he's had his day. The thing's misfired . . , a flop. Tear down the bills." Destroy the idol.

When my father went to Harrow at fourteen the first thing that happened to him was to be made to stand up, in class, while the rest of the boys stared at him for having a famous *Punch* artist for a parent. This was in 1887. When I went to finishing school in Paris in 1925 the girls goggled round me because I was Gerald du Maurier's daughter. There is a lad at school in 1958 who gets chaffed and ragged because he is Daphne du Maurier's son. A circus family has no illusions about success. They tumble from the cradle, and are used to taking knocks. It is the amateur and the dilettante who hide their heads in shame when the jeers begin; or, swift to offence, hit back in anger.

If fan letters do not surprise me, or begging letters either, it is because I read my father's and my grandfather's as wall. The people who write these letters are sincere, but they are lonely. They are writing to an idol, to a myth—never to an individual. Sometimes, answering them, I have wondered what would happen if I followed up my acknowledgement with a ring on the bell, a knock on the door, and a request, "You said you wished you knew me. Here I am. May I share your home?" What bewildered stares! What stammering denials!

If those of us who have been successful with what wares we peddle are truly honest, we will admit a certain snob value to praise. The college girl who empties her heart from Texas is tossed aside more quickly than the poet from Corfu. The old lady who knew an aunt in Cambridge is answered, reluctantly, on Friday, but that fellow author we so much admire, and find to our delight and gratification admires us too, he is answered the very afternoon that his letter came.

Vanity, vanity, all is vanity, said the preacher, except during that moment when the writer felt the flash and wrote . . . what did he write? The flash has gone. It's as swift as that, as ephemeral, as fierce, but, like the song that ended, the memory lingers on.

Quite otherwise the trappings. I remember coming out of the underground in Piccadilly. I was alone, it was raining, and I had no date for the evening and very little money on me, not enough for a taxi. I looked up and saw my name in lights, and the title of the current film, *Rebecca*. There were lines of people standing in a queue, waiting to go in. I did not join them. Moments of success? Perhaps.

ROMANTIC LOVE

There is no such thing as romantic love. This is a statement of fact, and I defy all those who hold a contrary opinion. Romantic love is an illusion, a name given to cover up an illicit relationship between two people, one of whom is married, or betrothed, to somebody else. The great love stories of the world that have been handed down to us through the centuries, whether in verse or prose or sung upon a lute, have had for theme forbidden passion, for nothing else would stimulate the reader, or in earlier days hold the attention of the listener, as he or she sat before the hearth and waited upon the teller of old tales. Battles, yes, the gorier the better, slaughter, blood, Hector dragged round the walls of Troy; but Helen was the prime cause, who left her husband Menelaus of her own free will and fled with her lover Paris, son of the Trojan King Priam. If ever illicit love brought disaster in its train this did, some twelve hundred years B.C., causing the deaths of thousands, Greeks and Trojans. Her lover Paris slain in battle, the beautiful Hellen returned to her husband Menelaus, and at his death retired to the island of Rhodes, where she was almost immediately strangled by order of her one-time friend Polyxo.

Romantic love? If so, a bloody business, with unhappiness for all.

Theseus, King of Athens, was one of the most celebrated heroes of antiquity, but he was no romantic lover, unless making love to two sisters at the same time can be called romantic. He eloped with Ariadne, elder daughter of the

90

King of Crete, to Naxos, and then deserted her and married her younger sister Phaedra. She, in due course, succumbed to a hopeless passion for Hippolytus, the son of Theseus by a former marriage; and because he did not return the love of his stepmother she accused him of rape, when he fled to the seashore and was drowned in his own chariot by a great wave which Neptune, in answer to Theseus' prayer, caused to rise up from the sea. On hearing of his death Phaedra hanged herself. A charming relationship.

Theseus, her husband, not content with one abduction in his life, invaded the underworld and tried to carry off the Queen of Hades but, foiled in the attempt by the god Pluto, King of Hades, he returned to Athens to find a usurper in charge, and then, lacking a family and a kingdom, he retired to Scyros, where he fell to his death from a precipice.

These were the tales that stimulated our ancestors in bygone centuries, and if the loves of mortals palled they could always fall back upon the amours of their gods. Zeus, or Jupiter as the Romans called him, reigned in heaven—Olympus—with his consort Hera, Juno, but his appetite was prodigious, and nothing pleased him more than to adopt a disguise when making love to earthly beings. He impregnated Leda, wife of the King of Sparta, in the guise of a swan, and she brought forth two eggs, from which, as they cracked, emerged four children, Castor and Clytemnestra, Pollux and Helen.

Castor and Pollux are twin stars in the sky, you can see them any night when the sky is clear, and as for Helen, we already know what happened to her. Clytemnestra, if she lacked her sister Helen's beauty, had inherited her swan father's appetite, for while her husband Agamemnon was away at the Trojan wars she lived in sin with her cousin Aegysthus, and then when her husband returned murdered him, only to be slaughtered in her turn by their son Orestes.

These stories, savage, brutal, utterly amoral, are the foundation of our literary culture. They spread from Greece to Rome and so throughout Europe, and although the gods died their deeds lived after them. New stories arose, based upon the old, but the main themes were the same: illicit passion, betrayal, and a grim death for the lovers. The coming of Christianity may have changed the course of history, although the birth of a heavenly son to a virgin has a curious similarity to the Greek myth preceding it, but despite the Jewish tradition of devout and strict family life, which had a supreme influence on Christian morals, when it came to singing songs and telling tales the main theme was still illicit love.

Arthur and Guinever . . . Guinever who betrayed her husband King Arthur with the greatest knight of all the world, Sir Lancelot, as the old romances of the Round Table described him; Tristan, son, not nephew, of King Mark of Cornwall, who, sent to Ireland to fetch his father's bride, fell in love with her himself, and she with him, so bringing jealousy and despair to the father's heart. Is it possible that the Tristan story is really an adaptation from the Theseus, Phaedra and Hippolytus tale, handed down from singer to minstrel, from Greece to Gaul, from Gaul to Brittany and Cornwall? During the telling of it the theme has softened. Tristan has become nephew, not son, thus drawing a veil over the incest barrier. King Mark has become an aged, crusty old man, the two lovers Tristan and Isolde both young and innocent, sleeping, when they fled his wrath to the woods, with a drawn sword between them.

Not so originally. Béroul, the first Frenchman to take up the tale and make a poem from it, described the love affair with all the robust humour inherited from some

earlier source. King Mark sprinkles the bedroom floor with
flour so that Tristan, creeping to Isolde's bed, will leave his
traces there. Tristan, disguising himself as a pilgrim, waits
by a ford which the Queen and her retinue cannot pass,
and offers himself as carrier. Then, with the Queen upon
his shoulders, he stumbles in the mud, and they fall
together to make play with one another in the shallows,
and later the Queen can tell her husband the King, without speaking an untruth, that she has "lain" with no man
except a pilgrim.

This is true bawdy, and certainly not romance. Here was
the stuff that made our ancestors slap their thighs and roll
in their seats, but it did not serve at a later date. The
women demanded romance, as they continue to do today
in their novels and magazines, and, if they can get it, on
their television screens as well. Lovely Guinever, noble
Sir Lancelot! Gallant Tristan, unhappy sweet Isolde! They
couldn't help falling in love. It just happened to them.

Another famous pair of lovers were Paolo and Francesca. Francesca, married to a lame husband, Giovanni
Sciancato (John the Lame), falls in love with his younger
brother Paolo, but not, let me remind the reader, until
both the innocent young people are sitting together reading the story of Lancelot and Guinever. (Which proves
that reading about illicit love can corrupt the reader.)
Then, as the poet Dante has it, "*Noi leggiavamo un giorno
per diletto, di Lancialotto, come amor lo strinse!*" or, in
matter-of-fact prose, "One day we read of Lancelot, and
how love constrained him. We were alone, and without all
suspicion. Our eyes met, and when we read how the fond
smile was kissed by such a lover, he, who shall never be
divided from me, kissed my mouth all trembling." The
deed was done. Fate ran its course. John the Lame discovered what was brewing, and murdered both his wife and
younger brother.

Of course Dante, being a good Christian, a Catholic to boot, and not a Greek or Roman poet, had the two lovers condemned forever to circle on the winds in hell. You can read of them in the Inferno. And yes, Helen of Troy is there too, and Tristan, and other illicit lovers, including— but possibly she deserved it—Cleopatra, though Antony is not named. Dido is amongst the damned, simply because she killed herself for love after her husband's death—he was her uncle, incidentally—and this has always seemed to me a curious choice on Dante's part, because poor Dido had committed no ill need. Whether it was the suicide, or the marriage to the uncle, that caused Dante to shake his head I have never discovered. As for Paolo and Francesca, and the other band of doomed sinners, surely the Greeks would have turned them into stars? We lost much when Olympus fell.

Shakespeare, living three centuries after Dante, had a lighter touch with lovers. True, the jealous husband plays his customary role, and though Desdemona, unlike Isolde and Guinever, is innocent of adultery, her spouse Othello smothers her with a pillow. But then Shakespeare never claimed his play was a romance. *Othello* is a tragedy, and so is *Antony and Cleopatra*, in which Egypt's Queen (an inhabitant of Dante's Inferno) puts a poisonous snake to her bosom after her lover Antony has died of his wounds at her side. We may suppose, though we cannot say for certain, that there was much writhing and contortion, groans as well, upon the Elizabethan stage when the leading characters died. The spectators, pressing forward, would watch breathless as the boy actor, playing Cleopatra, put the asp to his breast and murmured, "Peace, peace! Dost thou not see my baby at my breast, That sucks the nurse asleep?" They were spared, probably from scenic difficulties, the drowning of mad Ophelia in *Hamlet*, but were told how "her garments, heavy with their drink,

Pull'd the poor wretch from her melodious lay To muddy death."

Shakespeare's most famous pair of lovers were undoubtedly Romeo and Juliet. Here at last, you will say, we have romance. Nothing illicit in this play, the tragic ending has us all in tears. Well . . . it must not be forgotten that in the first act Romeo declares himself burning wih love for one Rosaline, whom we are never permitted to see, alas; but for a young man supposedly suffering from a broken heart Romeo recovers very swiftly at first sight of Juliet. Juliet, at twelve years old, is equally stricken, but one wonders how much this mutual attraction between the two young people is whipped to a point of frenzied passion by the knowledge that any alliance would be forbidden by their shocked and horrified parents. Once more we have illicit love, and this makes the spice of the story, or did so at any rate for its Elizabethan audiences.

Had the course of true love run smooth, had Romeo and Juliet stood hand in hand a bridal pair in the final scene with Capulets and Montagues smiling, the whole point would have gone. Happy endings were implicit in Shakespeare's comedies, but these plays were mostly given before selected audiences, written for specific occasions, guests at court and so on, when, having dined well, the assembled company preferred to be soothed and entertained rather than horrified or stirred. Hence in *Twelfth Night* the jaded palate of the sophisticated visitor or courtier could be tickled by the spectacle of a lovesick duke becoming unconsciously attracted to a girl disguised as a page, with the widow for whom he has sighed in vain so long herself seeking the favours of the same supposed youth. Shakespeare, tongue in cheek, knew only too well what went on behind the scenes of Queen Elizabeth's court. The same sort of deception delighted those who watched *As You Like It*. Girls dressed as boys; Portia did it too in *The Merchant of Venice*. A fairy besotted by a fool with an ass's head was the final touch of irony spun in *A Midsummer Night's Dream*. Shakespeare was well aware that to make a comedy savoury you had to play it witty, coarse and quick, or you would have your audience on the yawn.

Therefore today, when we upbraid the modern playwright for pornography, let us remember that the tradition is long-standing, handed on by masters of the game, Aristophanes surely being the supreme example. They did it, however, with more finesse. To show lovers naked in the act would have dulled the appetite.

The great dramatists were never romantic, any more than the great novelists. Tolstoy did not portray a happy wife in *Anna Karenina*. She deceived her husband for a pretty worthless lover, and when he went to the wars preferred to throw herself under a train rather than live without him. Flaubert's Madame Bovary, bored with provincial life and her doctor husband, lacked courage at first to console herself with a lover, but when she succumbed to Rodolphe Boulanger and Léon Dupuis corruption set in, lies, deceit, debts, all sense of honour left her, and in the end, deserted by her lovers, her still-loving husband absent, she died a slow and painful death from self-administered arsenic. A fine romance.

Hardy's Tess of the D'Urbervilles was dogged by fate from the start. Raped by a man she did not love, then married to one she did, who spurned her on the wedding night when he learnt the secret from her own lips, she passed a wretched existence desired by the first, desiring the second, and in the end, having stabbed to death, while he slept, the man who had first possessed her, she ran away after her true husband Angel Clare, seeking forgiveness, which at last he gave, even for the murder, but it was too late for happiness. The officials of the law came to arrest her, and, as Hardy himself put it, the immortals had finished their sport with Tess. Here is the essence of Greek tragedy, but in nineteenth-century England.

Wuthering Heights has been acclaimed as a supreme romantic novel, but what is romantic about its hero Heathcliffe, who marries a woman he despises in order to ill-treat her and to spite her brother, who mistreats in equal measure the delicate son he has by her, and tries to turn this son's wife into a kitchen slut? And all this because Cathy, his foster sister and the only being in the world he has ever had feeling for, marries another and then dies in childbirth? There is more savagery, more brutality, in the pages of *Wuthering Heights* than in any novel of the nineteenth century, and, for good measure, more beauty too, more poetry, and, what is more unusual, a complete lack of sexual emotion. Heathcliffe's feeling for Cathy, Cathy's for Heathcliffe, despite their force and passion, have a non-sexual quality; the emotion is elemental like the wind on Wuthering Heights.

Emily Brontë, striding over the Yorkshire moors with her dog, did not conjure from her imagination any cosy tale of happy lovers to console women readers sitting snugly within doors. A romance, according to my dictionary, is a tale "with scenes and incidents remote from everyday life," and a romancer a "fantastic liar." Well, fair enough. If a romantic tale is what editors of magazines demand for their reading public they may get it, but not quite in the form for which they hoped: instead, jealousy, treachery, deceit, passion, ending all too often in a violent death. It is not, alas, the gods who make men and women mad, but the chemistry in the blood. "Men have died . . . and worms have eaten them, but not for love . . ."

THIS I BELIEVE

In my end is my beginning. The ill-fated Mary Stuart, Queen of France and of Scotland, chose this cryptic saying as her motto. It was embroidered, in French, upon her chair of state—*En ma fin est mon commencement*—a puzzle to those who looked upon it, but the truth was that the quotation came from a fourteenth-century lyric written by a priest, Giles de Machant, and the song doubtless took her fancy when she was young and gay and lived in France with her youthful husband the Dauphin, later François II, before she had any presentiment of his early death or of her own future tempestuous life and unhappy middle years.

We, knowing her history, remembering the blindfold figure stumbling towards the block, may venture to transpose the words and read into them greater significance—In my beginning is my end. Mary Stuart carried within her from birth the potential seeds of disruption, doom and tragedy; such were the qualities and traits inherited from her forebears that, no matter what road she had followed, and even if she had reigned neither in Scotland nor in France, she would have caused disunity and stress.

In our beginning is our end. The colour of our eyes, our skin, the shape of our hands, the depth of our emotions, the bump of humour or lack of it, the small talents we may put to good account, even the ill-health that suddenly in later life descends without apparent reason—these are the things that make us what we are. There is no cell in our bodies that has not been transmitted to us by our ancestors, and the very blood group to which we belong may predispose us to the disease that finally kills. We are all of us chemical particles, inherited not only from our parents but from a million ancestors; and because of this we beget in turn, passing on to our descendants at best a doubtful, sometimes a disturbing legacy.

I find these facts, of which I knew little in my youth, exciting, even exhilarating. They stand for order, for a plan. They make for sense in what too often in the past seemed a senseless world. If the particles that we now are came originally from an explosion in or near the sun, and the sun itself from yet another explosion in a kindred universe, then there is no limit either to the past or to the future, life of some sort is continuous, it has no beginning and no end. Our world may burn, disintegrate: there will be others. New explosions will form new particles, which will unite. Life will go on. Creation is at work, has always been at work, will always be at work.

The image of a super-Brain, sitting before a blueprint of a million universes and commanding, "Let there be light," does not convince me, nor that such a super-Brain should point a finger at the particle I am and demand subservience to its authority. The super-Brain, if it exists, has made too many errors of judgement through the ages to deem itself omnipotent, and so win our allegiance. The automaton that gives life has, like our own inventors, second and third thoughts when working out a problem. What cannot adapt is scrapped. The first insects, the first reptiles, were too large, too cumbersome. They became redundant. Giant bats with wings and claws that pawed the sky were mistakes and—to use a modern term—were quickly scrubbed, along with the lumbering mammals glimpsed by our first ancestors. Plants, fishes, birds, apes are tried, found wanting, vanish. Races die out. Civilisations crumble. Not because an Almighty Ruler deals out punishment to offending sinners, but because certain particles of matter have failed to adapt to the changing circumstances of a particular period.

I have never understood why this belief—for belief it is —cannot be reconciled with a firm faith in all the finer feelings and qualities that have evolved in man since he first stood erect. Self-preservation, the instinct to reproduce his species, was part of his genetic inheritance. He had to destroy to live, and by forming into tribes, into groups, achieve greater stability. Awareness of others, the feeling for his young shared by all birds and beasts, enabled him to keep his unit strong.

The bird that trails its wing to avert danger to its chick and deceives the pursuer, the lioness that guards its cub, the woman who snatches her child from the road on the approach of a car, these things are done from an agelong impulse to preserve the species, to adapt, to meet the future; and the chemical change that fires the impulse, the discharge of adrenalin into the bloodstream that directs the action, these are all part of our inheritance, transmuted from those first particles that gave us life. I do not see what all this has to do with God unless God is another name for Life—not omnipotent, not unchanging, but forever growing, forever developing, forever discarding old worlds and creating new ones.

If we are particles made to a repetitive pattern, our actions and our thoughts frequently predictable, no more able to change our pattern than a plant, cross-fertilised to bloom purple, will turn yellow, nevertheless we can come to terms with our inheritance, recognise the good within us, and the ill. As an individual living here and now I am only too well aware that I possess feelings, emotions, a mind and body bequeathed to me by people long since dead who have made me what I am. Generations of French craftsmen of the tight-knit glass-blowing fraternity, provincial, clannish, have handed on to me a strong family sense, a wary suspicion of all who are not "us". Drawing their life and sustenance from the deep forests of Vibraye and Montmirail, they have made me to their pattern, and thus inevitably, it seemed, I sought wooded shelter, the protection of great trees, for what ultimately came to be my home. Respect for tradition vies in me with a contempt for authority imposed from above, a legacy of French temperament passed on from that nation of individualists.

In my beginning is my end; and having passed through many phases and attempts to be other than I am, I have reached my fifty-eighth year with the realisation that basically I have never changed. The child who rebelled against parental standards rebels against them still in middle age. The sceptic of seven who queried the existence of God in the sky, of fairies in the woods, of Father Christmas descending every London chimney in a single magic night, remains a sceptic at fifty-seven, believing all things possible only when they can be proved by scientific fact. The child who avoided the company of adults, and of her own contemporaries with the exception of the immediate members of her family, preferring solitude in the countryside and an interchange of conversation with her own self, does so still. A hatred of injustice fills me now as it did then. Kindness seems to me the one quality worth praising, but today I give it a longer name and call it compassion.

I have known only one person in my life whom I would truly call good, and that was my maternal grandmother, a little woman of great simplicity and charm, who, when she entered a room, made it warm with her bright presence. English to the core, a native of the Cambridgeshire fens, "honest cathedral stock," as my father used to say in playful mockery of his mother-in-law, no adversity of circumstance defeated her. She was always smiling, always serene, the light and centre of her modest home. Kneeling beside her in St. Jude's Church, Golders Green—I would have been about nine and she in her late fifties—I remember watching her bowed head, her closed eyes, and the fervent movement of her lips as she murmured the words of the Confession at Morning Service, and the sight of such humility filled me with outrage against the vicar, against God, that both should deem it necessary for someone as gentle and as unselfish as my little grandmother to admit to uncommitted sin.

"We have followed too much the devices and desires of our own hearts. We have offended against thy holy laws. We have left undone those things which we ought to have done; and we have done those things which we ought not to have done; and there is no health in us. But thou, O Lord, have mercy upon us, miserable offenders . . ." The miserable offender was the final straw. If God demanded such self-abasement from one who brought only happiness to those about her, then I wanted no part of Him. I questioned, at that moment, all authority from heaven. I had no compulsion to obey God's holy laws. I was not a miserable offender any more than was my grandmother but, unlike her, I would not ask for mercy. As for sin, the word was meaningless. It is so still. The only sin then, as now, is cruelty, and today I know that cruelty is bred from ignorance out of fear.

Prayer is different, too habit-forming ever to be shed. I pray nightly upon my knees today as I did then, ending with the childish words, "Let everything be all right," as if, by so expressing myself, I may come to terms with fate. Yet I know in my heart that the only worthwhile prayer is a prayer for courage, courage to bear the ills that may come upon me, and the ills that I may bring upon myself. I know now that the good we do returns to us in full measure, and the evil that we do rebounds also—the lies, the deceits, the evasions which we have inflicted on other people.

Dante's Inferno is not so far from the truth. Hell is what we make it. The damned endure torment not from the underworld but from within. Hell is not other people, as Sartre would have it, but ourselves. We inflict our own punishment. Meanwhile centuries of civilisation have not yet devised a cure for crime. Society imprisons the criminal instead of directing his interest towards a panacea for the committed crime. It would be more humane, and might be more successful, to train those who assault the old and feeble to care for the sick and aged, to make the rapists of young women work as midwives, put the poisoners into laboratories to discover some means of saving life rather than destroying it.

There are certain fundamental laws which have helped to shape us as human beings from the earliest days, and without which we should perish. The strongest of these is the law of the family unit, the binding together of a man and a woman to produce children. In the process of time this may become unnecessary, the test-tube baby turn out to be a more practical, less wasteful method of begetting and rearing the young. In our present state of development we cannot do without the unit. Emotionally, we should be starved. We seek, even in the sexual act, a long-lost comfort. A basic peace, reunion with ourselves. The fact that marriages so often fail is our misfortune. Incest being denied us, we must make do with second best. The perfect husband or wife is an illusion, a hero or a heroine born of fantasy, something we seldom recognise until, as Hamlet phrased it, the heyday in the blood is tame.

Society, as we know it, must disintegrate once the family dissolves. Nothing but the family bond will hold men and women together. Already women, emerging from centuries of submission, fret against their more passive role, demanding equality in all things as their right, but in achieving this they lose their first purpose in life, which is to preserve, to maintain the family. Women have not yet learnt how to serve their families and their own ambitions without conflict, and until they do so husband and children suffer, as well as they themselves. This is the greatest problem of our time. Our own and succeeding generations must learn to adjust to the ever changing status of women in our modern civilisation, for without a home, without a centre, we become disoriented, lost orphans without shelter, faith and confidence collapsing about us like a house of cards. Chaos reigns.

The second great problem of our time is how to live without religion. I believe that the dawn of the religious instinct in man came about through his first encounter with death. Death which slew his father and his mother, so that his groping mind sought consolation in a greater Father, a greater Mother, whether in the sky or in the bowels of the earth. He saw disease or misadventure strike down the beings upon whom he had hitherto depended. He saw them wither and grow old. This could not be. Therefore he created in his imagination the immortal ones. They would never let him down. The eternal Father would command him, praise him, punish him, the eternal Mother nourish him. Whatever he could not understand was of their doing. The laws of his own parents became confused with the sterner laws of his gods, and the necessity for sacrifice arose. The earthly parents, those frail creatures who grew old and died, losing all strength and beauty by so doing, were then transformed into immortals too. They lived on, but in another sphere, in the Islands of the Blest, or beyond the stars. Death, the last enemy, was thus defeated.

Belief in gods and demons became ingrained. The gods were good, the demons evil. Man was the tool of both, torn in conflict by opposing wills. The necessity to worship, to do homage to something greater than ourselves, is bred in the bone. It is part of our heritage, irrevocably intertwined with the basic need for family, for security. Deprived of our gods, of God, we are children without parents, hungry, lonely, fearful of the dark. Mankind, in this present century, balks dogma, balks what our fore-fathers called Divine Authority. Yet if those we revere on earth deceive us, to whom then shall we turn?

There is a faculty amongst the myriad threads of our in-heritance that, unlike the chemicals in our bodies and in our brains, has not yet been pinpointed by science, or even fully examined. I like to call this faculty the sixth sense. It is a sort of seeing, a sort of hearing, something between perception and intuition, an indefinable grasp of things un-known. Psychologists have called this sense the Uncon-scious Mind, the Superego, the Psyche, the Self. Scientists, to date, are not prepared to acknowledge such a sense, or, when they do, explain it as a memory storehouse, connect-ed to the brain. This may well be, but, whether it proves so or not, it is also a storehouse of potential power. The phenomena of precognition, of telepathy, of dreaming true, all come from this storehouse, and the therapeutic value of hypnosis, still in its infancy, depends upon it too. The sixth sense, latent in young children, animals and primitive peoples, more highly developed in the East than in the West, has long lain dormant in most civilised societies.

I believe that neglect of this sixth sense has contributed to our problems throughout the ages. It can act as guide, as mentor, warning us of danger, signalling caution, yet also urging us to new discoveries. This untapped source of power, this strange and sometimes mystical intuitive sense, may come to be, generations hence, mankind's salvation. If we can communicate, one with another, by thought alone, if a message from the storehouse can act as a panacea to pain, so curing the body's suffering, if recognition of a fault, a crime, can be understood before it is committed, if dreaming in time can recapture from the past certain events known to our forebears but unperceived by us, then surely a series of possibilities, multitudinous, astonishing, may lie ahead for our children's children.

Naturally there is danger in the use of the sixth sense. There is danger in the misuse of electricity, of atomic power: dabblers in magic, in the occult, in so-called spiritualism (telepathy in another guise) and the quack hypnotists, all can use the sixth sense to their own advantage. The combat between the good within us and the evil will always be with us. It is again part of our inheritance. The serpent under the tree, the demons from Pandora's box, these figments of our doubts and fears will continue to threaten us until they are perceived and understood. Each one of us is Perseus, who, cutting off Medusa's head, saw her reflection in the mirror and recognised himself. The sixth sense can help us to this recognition and, by fusing the conscious with the unconscious, broaden our vision so that all things become possible. When Jesus said, "The kingdom of God is within you," I believe he meant just this. As prophet and seer, with the sixth sense more highly developed possibly than in anyone before his time or since, he knew the potentialities of the inner power and drew upon it, believing, as one of Jewish faith, that the source was Yahweh.

The gospels, their message blurred though beautiful, show us a messianic figure of compelling personality at once loved and often misunderstood by his immediate followers, speaking in riddles. Was the historical Jesus, the healer of the sick, the worker of miracles, the opposer of buying and selling in the Temple, more deeply involved in a struggle to help the oppressed peoples of Israel than we have hitherto been told? Can the shouts of the populace calling "Hosanna . . . Hosanna . . ." in that fateful Passover week be interpreted as "Free us . . . Free us . . ."? Did that cry of agony from the cross, in Aramaic *"Eli, Eli, lama shabachthani*," mean "My power, my power, why have you gone from me"?

This, to the devout Christian, will seem blasphemy, a denial of all later teaching, reducing the Son of God to the Son of Man. Yet the cry of Jesus, however it was phrased, was the eternal question put by man in the face of death since the beginning of time. No answer from the heavens. No answer from within. The historical Jesus nailed to his cross, the mythical Prometheus chained to his rock, both dared to refashion men on earth by breathing fire upon them, to turn them from figures of clay and matter into living gods. Their failure was their glory. For only by daring can man evolve, shake himself free, triumph over the hereditary shackles that bind him to his own species. Only by daring can the spirit, hitherto a prisoner in matter, break away from the body's ties, travel at will across time and space, discarding the body's aids that have served in ages past, the eyes, the ears, the heart, the lungs, and venture into the unknown, untrammelled, free.

Nothing is impossible, no vision too distorted that cannot become reality generations hence. A hundred years ago men would have laughed to scorn the idea that, sitting at home in their armchairs, they might watch and hear events taking place thousands of miles away, that they themselves could travel in a few hours across the sky from one end of the globe to the other, that drugs would combat madness and disease, that atomic power would bring light or destruction to whole continents, that their great-great-grandchildren might land upon the moon. Man is forever seeking, forever probing, and although as individual particles we must conform to a pattern, to a design, the great process of adaptation still continues, changing us imperceptibly, so that we cannot foresee what we shall ultimately become.

In my beginning is my end. The I who writes this essay

lives and dies. Something of myself goes into the children born of my body, and to their children, and those children's children. Life, whatever shape or form it takes, goes on, develops, adapts.

Humbert Wolfe, a poet of my youth now dead and seldom, so I am told, read by the young of today, wrote a long poem, first published in 1930, called *The Uncelestial City*. Three verses caught my attention in those days, over thirty years ago, not particularly for their language but for the attitude expressed, and they sum up for me now, as they did then, all that I have been trying to say in the foregoing pages.

> Continue! knowing as the pine-trees know
>   that somewhere in the urgent sap there is
> an everlasting answer to the snow
>   and a retort to the last precipice,
>
> that, merely by climbing, the shadow is made less,
>   that we have some engagement with a star
> only to be honoured by death's bitterness,
>   and where the inaccessible godheads are,
>
> that to plunge upwards is the way of the spark,
>   and that, burning up and out, even as we die
> we challenge and dominate the shameless dark
>   with our gold death—and that is my reply.

DEATH AND WIDOWHOOD

[1966]

Death, to the novelist, is a familiar theme. Often it is the high spot of a particular tale, turning romance to tragedy. A character, his demise planned for a certain chapter while the story was still in notebook form, vanishes from the manuscript, and the author, like a successful murderer whose victim has disappeared, decides that the killing was well done. I have done this several times in my novels. I can even confess I enjoyed the killing. It gave a certain zest to the writing, and if I felt an inward pang for the loss of the character I had created, the pang was soon forgotten and the memory faded. The fictitious person was, after all, only a puppet of my imagination, and I could create others to take his place. The writer, like a spider, spins a web; the creatures caught in the web have no substance, no reality.

It is only when death touches the writer in real life that he, or she, realises the full impact of its meaning. The deathbed scene, described so often in the past, with fingers tapping it out upon a typewriter or pen scratching it on paper, becomes suddenly true. The shock is profound. Sometimes this encounter with reality can so awaken the writer from the imaginary world that he never recovers. I believe that this is what happened to Emily Brontë. The fantasy world of Gondal that had been hers, peopled with heaven knows how many persons, coupled with the harsher, wilder land of Heathcliffe, Cathy and *Wuthering*

Heights, faded on a certain Sunday morning when her brother Branwell, his dragging illness accepted with resignation for so long, of a sudden died. A cold, caught at his funeral and then neglected, hastened her own decline and death barely three months afterwards. It does not account for her stubborn refusal to see a doctor, her silence with her two sisters, her complete withdrawal within herself, which can only be explained by shock, or trauma as we would call it today, occasioned by direct experience of death. The death of a brother, for which she blamed her sisters and herself. They had neglected him. Therefore, she argued, she must be neglected likewise. It was an unconscious form of suicide, not uncommon to the suddenly bereaved.

I am a writer too. Neither a poet nor a great romantic novelist like Emily Brontë, but a spinner of webs, a weaver of imaginary tales; and when my husband died in March of this past year it was as though the sheltered cloudland that had enveloped me for years, peopled with images drawn from my imagination, suddenly dissolved, and I was face to face with a harsh and terrible reality. The husband I had loved and taken for granted for thirty-three years of married life, father of my three children, lay dead. If by writing about it now I expose myself and my feelings, it is not from a sense of self-advertisement, but because by doing so I may be able to help those readers who, like myself, have suffered the same sense of shock.

Like Emily Brontë, one of my first reactions, after the first bewildered fits of weeping, was to blame myself. I could have done more during the last illness, I should have observed, with sharp awareness, the ominous signs. I should have known, the last week, the last days, that his eyes followed me with greater intensity, and instead of moving about the house on trivial business, as I did, should never have left his side. How heartless, in retrospect, my last good night, when he murmured to me, "I can't sleep," and I kissed him and said, "You will, darling, you will," and went from the room. Perhaps, if I had sat with him all night, the morning would have been otherwise. As it was, when morning came, and the nurses who had shared his vigil expressed some anxiety about his pallor and asked me to telephone the doctor, I went through to him expecting possibly an increase of weakness, but inevitably the usual smile. Instead . . . he turned his face to me, and died.

My readers will have heard of the kiss of life. We tried it, the nurses and myself, in turn until the doctor came. But I knew, as I breathed into his body, that it was useless and he was dead. His eyes were open but the spark had gone. What had been living was no more. This, then, was the finality of death. Described by myself in books time without number. Experienced at last.

The aftermath of shock must alter the chemistry in the blood, for it forced me to action instead of to collapse. I had to telephone my children. Make arrangements. See that necessary things were done. These responses were automatic, numb. Part of my brain functioned, part of it seemed closed. The part of it that was automatic and dissociated from emotion ordered an immediate autopsy so that the doctor's first assessment of death by sudden coronary thrombosis could be verified. The part of it that was numb began to fuse with the emotions, every instinct urging me to perform those actions he would have wished carried out, the wording to *The Times* making clear that by his own request the cremation should be private, there would be no memorial service, instead his friends might send donations to the Security Fund for Airborne Forces —those Airborne Forces he had commanded in 1942, 1943 and 1944, his beloved "paras," his glider pilots.

It was not until the cremation was over, which only my children and a few close friends attended, and I had scattered my husband's ashes at the end of the garden where we often walked together, and my children had returned to their own homes, that I knew, with full force, the finality of death. I was alone. The newly discovered tenderness of my daughters, the sudden maturity of my son, himself to become a father within a few months, had not prevailed upon me to go back with one of them, to recover, as they put it, from the strain. "No," I told them, "I want to face the future here, in my own home, by myself." To go elsewhere, even with them, would postpone the moment of truth. What had to be endured must be endured now, and at once, alone.

In marriage one partner—unless both are killed simultaneously—must go before the other. Usually the man goes first. Generations of wives have known this. Now I knew it too, and must adapt. I must force myself to look upon the familiar things, the coat hanging on the chair, the hat in the hall, the motoring gloves, the stick, the pile of yachting magazines beside his bed, and remind myself that this was not the separation of war that we had known twenty years earlier, but separation for all time.

To ease the pain I took over some of his things for myself. I wore his shirts, sat at his writing desk, used his pens to acknowledge the hundreds of letters of condolence; and, by the very process of identification with the objects he had touched, felt the closer to him. The evenings were the hardest to bear, the ritual of the hot drink, the lumps of sugar for the two dogs, the saying of prayers—his boyhood habit carried on throughout our married life—the good night kiss. I continued the ritual, because this too lessened pain, and was, in its very poignancy, a consolation.

I wept often because I could not prevent the tears, and possibly, in some way beyond my understanding, tears helped the healing process, but the physical act of weeping was distressing to me beyond measure. As a child I seldom cried.

I thought long and often about the possibility of life after death. Baptised and confirmed in the Christian faith, I acknowledge no denomination, yet have an instinctive yearning for survival, as indeed the human race has always done, since man first sought to come to terms with death. I liked to think of my husband reunited with the parents who had gone before him, and with his comrades of two world wars. I liked to think that all pain, all suffering, had been wiped out, that he knew, as none of us can know here on earth, indescribable joy, the "peace which passes all understanding"—a line he used to quote.

Yet I had seen his empty shell. I had seen the light flicker and go out. Where had it gone? Was it blown to emptiness after all, like the light of a candle, and does each one of us, in the end, vanish into darkness? If this is so, and our dreams of survival after death are only dreams, then we must accept this too. Not with fear and dismay, but with courage. To have lived at all is a measure of immortality; for a baby to be born, to become a man, a woman, to beget others like himself, is an act of faith in itself, even an act of defiance. It is as though every human being born into this world burns, for a brief moment, like a star, and because of it a pinpoint of light shines in the darkness, and so there is glory, so there is life. If there is nothing more than this, we have achieved our immortality.

Meanwhile, for the bereaved, who will never know the answer here on earth, the practical living of day-by-day continues. We must rise in the morning, eat, go about our business, watch the seasons pass, our life no longer shared. To plan for one, instead of two, brings a sense of apathy. Instinct says, "Why bother? What can the future hold?" The sense of urgency is lacking. A younger woman, with a family to rear, would be spurred by necessity to action. The older woman has no such driving force. Her children are adult, they can fend for themselves. The older woman must seek her reason for living either in outward forms—

good works, committees, the demanding tasks of a career —or look inward, deep within herself, for a new philosophy.

"At least," said a kind, well-wishing friend, "you have your writing," as though, with a magic wand, I could conjure at will a host of dancing puppets to grimace and do my bidding, their very antics proving an antidote to pain. Yes, I have my writing, but the stories that I fashioned once were fairy tales, and they cannot satisfy me now. Death, surely, will make me more aware of other people's suffering, of other people's ills, of the countless women there must be who, widowed like myself, have no form of consolation from without or from within. Some lack children, sisters, friends; others are financially bereft; a vast number lived in their husband's shadow, and with the shadow gone feel themselves not fully individuals, unwanted and ignored. What life can these women make for themselves, how will they adapt?

The widow, like the orphan, has been an object of pity from earliest times. She received charity. She lived, very often, with her married son or daughter, and earned, sometimes rightly, the hostility of her daughters- or sons-in-law. Her place was the chimney corner, and in more modern times the little flat upstairs or the bungalow next door.

The Hindu woman, in old days, committed suttee. She laid herself on the funeral pyre of her husband and was burnt with him. This was one way out of her dilemma. My own grandmother, widowed at the same age as myself, at fifty-eight, entered upon old age with grace and dignity. She donned her weeds and her widow's cap, and I can see her now, a kindly, grave, if rather formidable figure, endeavouring to teach me, a child, how to knit, in the First World War.

I look down today at my own weeds, dark slacks, a

white pullover, and I wonder if the change in garb is basic, a symbol of woman's emancipation, or simply a newer fashion, while fundamentally the widow's sense of loss remains unchanged. No matter how brave a face she puts upon her status, the widow is still a lonely figure, belonging nowhere, resembling in some indefinable manner the coloured races in a world dominated by whites. The attitude of the non-widowed is kindly, hearty, a little over-cheerful in the attempt to show the bereaved that nothing is different, just as the liberal white will shake his black brother by the hand, smiling broadly, to emphasise equality. Neither is deceived. Both are embarrassed. The widow, aware of her inadequacy, retires into her shell, while the other, dreading the floodgates of emotion, beats a hasty retreat. Carried to extremes, the division results in apartheid, the widowed and the non-widowed withdraw to their separate worlds, and there is no communion between the two.

The old adage, Time heals all wounds, is only true if there is no suppuration within. To be bitter, to lament unceasingly, "Why did this have to happen to him?" makes the wound fester; the mind, renewing the stab, causes the wound to bleed afresh. It is hard, very hard, not to be bitter in the early days, not to blame doctors, hospitals, drugs, that failed to cure. Harder still for the woman whose husband died not by illness but by accident, who was cut short in full vigour, in the prime of life, killed perhaps in a car crash returning home from work. The first instinct is to seek revenge upon the occupants of the other car, themselves unhurt, whose selfish excess of speed caused the disaster. Yet this is no answer to grief. All anger, all reproach, turns inwards upon itself. The infection spreads, pervading the mind and body.

I would say to those who mourn—and I can only speak from my own experience—look upon each day that comes as a challenge, as a test of courage. The pain will come in waves, some days worse than others, for no apparent reason. Accept the pain. Do not suppress it. Never attempt to hide grief from yourself. Little by little, just as the deaf, the blind, the handicapped develop with time an extra sense to balance disability, so the bereaved, the widowed, will find new strength, new vision, born of the very pain and loneliness which seem, at first, impossible to master. I address myself more especially to the middle-aged who, like myself, look back to over thirty years or more of married life and find it hardest to adapt. The young must, of their very nature, heal sooner than ourselves.

We know, and must face it honestly, that life for us can never be the same again. Marriage was not just another love affair, an episode, but the greater half of our existence. We can never give to another what we gave to the partner who has gone. All that is over, finished. And the years that lie ahead, ten, twenty, perhaps even thirty, must be travelled alone. This is a challenge, just as marriage, in the first place, was a challenge.

I remember on our wedding day, in July 1932, the good priest who married us drawing a comparison between the little boat in which we were to set forth on our honeymoon and marriage itself. "You will embark," he said, "on a fair sea, and at times there will be fair weather, but not always. You will meet storms and overcome them. You will take it in turns to steer your boat through fair weather and foul. Never lose courage. Safe harbour awaits you both in the end."

Today I remember this advice with gratitude. Even if I must, of necessity, steer my boat alone, I shall not, so I trust, lose my bearings but, because of all I have learnt through the past three-and-thirty years, with my fellow helmsman at my side, come eventually to my journey's end.

One final word to my contemporaries. Take time to plan your future. Do not let your relatives or friends, anxious for your welfare, push you into some hasty move that later you may regret. If it is financially possible for you, stay in your own home, with the familiar things about you. We need many months to become reconciled to the loss that has overtaken us; and if at first the silence of the empty house may seem unbearable, do not forget it is still the home you shared, which two persons made their own.

As the months pass and the seasons change, something of tranquillity descends, and although the well-remembered footstep will not sound again, nor the voice call from the room beyond, there seems to be about one in the air an atmosphere of love, a living presence. I say this in no haunting sense, ghosts and phantoms are far from my mind. It is as though one shared, in some indefinable manner, the freedom and the peace, even at times the joy, of another world where there is no more pain. It is not a question of faith or of belief. It is not necessary to be a follower of any religious doctrine to become aware of what I mean. It is not the prerogative of the devout. The feeling is simply there, pervading all thought, all action. When Christ the healer said, "Blessed are they that mourn, for they shall be comforted," he must have meant just this.

Later, if you go away, if you travel, even if you decide to make your home elsewhere, the spirit of tenderness, of love, will not desert you. You will find that it has become part of you, rising from within yourself; and because of it you are no longer fearful of loneliness, of the dark, because death, the last enemy, has been overcome.

THE HOUSE OF SECRETS

[1946]

It was an afternoon in late autumn, the first time I tried to find the house. October, November, the month escapes me. But in the west country autumn can make herself a witch, and place a spell upon the walker. The trees were golden brown, the hydrangeas had massive heads still blue and untouched by flecks of wistful grey, and I would set forth at three of an afternoon with foolish notions of August still in my head. "I will strike inland," I thought, "and come back by way of the cliffs, and the sun will yet be high, or at worst touching the horizon beyond the western hills."

Of course, I was still a newcomer to the district, a summer visitor, whose people had but lately bought the old "Swiss Cottage", as the locals called it, a name which, to us, had horrid associations with an underground railway in the Finchley Road at home.

We were not yet rooted. We were new folk from London. We walked as tourists walked, seeing what should be seen. So my sister and I, poring over an old guidebook, first came upon the name of Menabilly. What description the guidebook gave I cannot now remember, except that the house had been first built in the reign of Queen Elizabeth, that the grounds and woods had been in the last century famous for their beauty, and that the property had never changed hands from the time it came into being, but had passed down, in the male line, to the present owner.

Three miles from the harbour, easy enough to find; but what about keepers and gardeners, chauffeurs and barking dogs? My sister was not such an inveterate trespasser as I. We asked advice. "You'll find no dogs at Menabilly, nor any keepers either," we were told, "the house is all shut up. The owner lives in Devon. But you'll have trouble in getting there. The drive is nearly three miles long, and overgrown."

I for one was not to be deterred. The autumn colours had me bewitched before the start. So we set forth, Angela more reluctant, with a panting pekinese held by a leash. We came to the lodge at four turnings, as we had been told, and opened the creaking iron gates with the flash courage and appearance of bluff common to the trespasser. The lodge was deserted. No one peered at us from the windows. We slunk away down the drive, and were soon hidden by the trees. Is it really nigh on twenty years since I first walked that hidden drive and saw the beech trees, like the arches of a great cathedral, form a canopy above my head? I remember we did not talk, or if we did we talked in whispers. That was the first effect the woods had upon both of us.

The drive twisted and turned in a way that I described many years afterwards, when sitting at a desk in Alexandria and looking out upon a hard glazed sky and dusty palm trees; but on that first autumnal afternoon, when the drive was new to us, it had the magic quality of a place hitherto untrodden, unexplored. I was Scott in the Antarctic. I was Cortez in Mexico. Or possibly I was none of these things, but a trespasser in time. The woods were sleeping now, but who, I wondered, had ridden through them once? What hoofbeats had sounded and then died away? What carriage wheels had rolled and vanished? Doublet and hose. Boot and jerkin. Patch and powder. Stock and patent leather. Crinoline and bonnet.

The trees grew taller and the shrubs more menacing. Yet still the drive led on, and never a house at the end of it. Suddenly Angela said, "It's after four . . . and the sun's gone." The pekinese watched her, pink tongue lolling. And then he stared into the bushes, pricking his ears at nothing. The first owl hooted . . . .

"I don't like it," said Angela firmly. "Let's go home."

"But the house," I said with longing, "we haven't seen the house."

She hesitated, and I dragged her on. But in an instant the day was gone from us. The drive was a muddied path, leading nowhere, and the shrubs, green no longer but a shrouding black, turned to fantastic shapes and sizes. There was not one owl now, but twenty. And through the dark trees, with a pale grin upon his face, came the first glimmer of the livid hunter's moon.

I knew then that I was beaten. For that night only.

"All right," I said grudgingly, "we'll find the house another time."

And, following the moon's light, we struck through the trees and came out upon the hillside. In the distance below us stretched the sea. Behind us the woods and the valley through which we had come. But nowhere was there a sign of any house. Nowhere at all.

"Perhaps," I thought to myself, "it is a house of secrets, and has no wish to be disturbed." But I knew I should not rest until I had found it.

If I remember rightly the weather broke after that day, and the autumn rains were upon us. Driving rain, day after day. And we, not yet become acclimatized to Cornish wind and weather, packed up and returned to London for the winter. But I did not forget the woods of Menabilly, or the house that waited . . . .

We came back again to Cornwall in the spring, and I was seized with a fever for fishing. I would be out in a boat most days, with a line in the water, and it did not matter much what came on the end of it, whether it would be seaweed or a dead crab, as long as I could sit on the thwart of a boat and hold a line and watch the sea. The boatman sculled off the little bay called Pridmouth, and as I looked at the land beyond, and saw the massive trees climbing from the valley to the hill, the shape of it all seemed familiar.

"What's up there, in the trees?" I said.

"That's Menabilly," came the answer, "but you can't see the house from the shore. It's away up yonder. I've never been there myself." I felt a bite on my line at that moment and said no more. But the lure of Menabilly was upon me once again.

Next morning I did a thing I had never done before, nor ever did again, except once in the desert, where to see sunrise is the peak of all experience. In short, I rose at 5.00 a.m. I pulled across the harbour in my pram, walked through the sleeping town, and climbed out upon the cliffs just as the sun himself climbed out on Pont Hill behind me. The sea was glass. The air was soft and misty warm. And the only other creature out of bed was a fisherman, hauling crab pots at the harbour mouth. It gave me a fine feeling of conceit, to be up before the world. My feet in sand shoes seemed like wings. I came down to Pridmouth Bay, passing the solitary cottage by the lake, and, opening a small gate hard by, I saw a narrow path leading to the woods. Now, at last, I had the day before me, and no owls, no moon, no shadows could turn me back.

I followed the path to the summit of the hill and then, emerging from the woods, turned left, and found myself upon a high grass walk, with all the bay stretched out below me and the Gribben head beyond.

I paused, stung by the beauty of that first pink glow of sunrise on the water, but the path led on, and I would not be deterred. Then I saw them for the first time—the scarlet rhododendrons. Massive and high they reared above my head, shielding the entrance to a long smooth lawn. I was hard upon it now, the place I sought. Some instinct made me crouch upon my belly and crawl softly to the wet grass at the foot of the shrubs. The morning mist was lifting, and the sun was coming up above the trees even as the moon had done last autumn. This time there was no owl, but blackbird, thrush and robin greeting the summer day.

I edged my way on to the lawn, and there she stood. My house of secrets. My elusive Menabilly . . .

The windows were shuttered fast, white and barred. Ivy covered the grey walls and threw tendrils round the windows. The house, like the world, was sleeping too. But later, when the sun was high, there would come no wreath of smoke from the chimneys. The shutters would not be thrown back, or the doors unfastened. No voices would sound within those darkened rooms. Menabilly would sleep on, like the sleeping beauty of the fairy tale, until someone should come to wake her.

I watched her awhile in silence, and then became emboldened, and walked across the lawn and stood beneath the windows. The scarlet rhododendrons encircled her lawns, to south, to east, to west. Behind her, to the north, were the tall trees and the deep woods. She was a two-storied house, and with the ivy off her would have a classical austerity that her present shaggy covering denied her.

One of her nineteenth-century owners had taken away her small-paned windows and given her plate glass instead, and he had also built at her northern end an ugly wing that conformed ill with the rest of her. But with all her faults, most obvious to the eye, she had a grace and charm that made me hers upon the instant. She was, or so it seemed to me, bathed in a strange mystery. She held a secret—not one, not two, but many—that she withheld from many people but would give to one who loved her well.

As I sat on the edge of the lawn and stared at her I felt as many romantic, foolish people have felt about the Sphinx. Here was a block of stone, even as the desert Sphinx, made by man for his own purpose—yet she had a personality that was hers alone, without the touch of human hand. One family only had lived within her walls. One family who had given her life. They had been born there, they had loved, they had quarrelled, they had suffered, they had died. And out of these emotions she had woven a personality for herself, she had become what their thoughts and their desires had made her.

And now the story was ended. She lay there in her last sleep. Nothing remained for her but to decay and die . . . .

I cannot recollect, now, how long I lay and stared at her. It was past noon, perhaps, when I came back to the living world. I was empty and lightheaded, with no breakfast inside me. But the house possessed me from that day, even as a mistress holds her lover.

Ours was a strange relationship for fifteen years. I would put her from my mind for months at a time, and then, on coming again to Cornwall, I would wait a day or two, then visit her in secret.

Once again I would sit on the lawn and stare up at her windows. Sometimes I would find that the caretaker at the lodge, who came now and again to air the house, had left a blind pulled back, showing a chink of space, so that by pressing my face to the window I could catch a glimpse of a room. There was one room—a dining room, I judged, because of the long sideboard against the wall—that held my fancy most. Dark panels. A great fireplace. And on the walls the family portraits stared into the silence and the dust. Another room, once a library, judging by the books upon the shelves, had become a lumber place, and in the centre of it stood a great dappled rocking horse with scarlet nostrils. What little blue-sashed, romping children once bestrode his back? Where was the laughter gone? Where were the voices that had called along the passages?

One autumn evening I found a window unclasped in the ugly north wing at the back. It must have been intuition that made me bring my torch with me that day. I threw open the creaking window and climbed in. Dust. Dust everywhere. The silence of death. I flashed my torch on to the cobwebbed walls and walked the house. At last. I had imagined it so often. Here were the rooms, leading from one to another, that I had pictured only from outside. Here was the staircase, and the faded crimson wall. There the long drawing room, with its shiny chintz sofas and chairs, and here the dining room, a forgotten corkscrew still lying on the sideboard.

Suddenly the shadows became too many for me, and I turned and went back the way I had come. Softly I closed the window behind me. And as I did so, from a broken pane on the floor above my head came a great white owl, who flapped his way into the woods and vanished . . . .

Some shred of convention still clinging to my nature turned me to respectability. I would not woo my love in secret. I wrote to the owner of the house and asked his permission to walk about his grounds. The request was granted. Now I could tread upon the lawns with a slip of paper in my pocket to show my good intentions, and no longer crawl belly to the ground like a slinking thief.

Little by little, too, I gleaned snatches of family history. There was the lady in blue who looked, so it was said, from a side window, yet few had seen her face. There was the cavalier found beneath the buttress wall more than a hundred years ago. There were the sixteenth-century builders, merchants and traders; there were the Stuart royalists, who suffered for their king; the Tory landowners with their white wigs and their brood of children; the Victorian garden lovers with their rare plants and their shrubs.

I saw them all, in my mind's eye, down to the present owner, who could not love his home; and when I thought of him it was not of an elderly man, a respectable justice of the peace, but of a small boy orphaned at two years old, coming for his holidays in an Eton collar and tight black suit, watching his old grandfather with nervous, doubtful eyes. The house of secrets. The house of stories.

The war came, and my husband and I were now at Hythe in Kent, and many miles from Cornwall. I remember a letter coming from my sister.

"By the way, there is to be a sale at Menabilly. Everything to be sold up, and the house just left to fall to bits. Do you want anything?"

Did I want anything? I wanted her, my house. I wanted every stick of furniture, from the Jacobean oak to the Victorian bamboo. But what was the use? The war had come. There was no future for man, woman or child. And anyway, Menabilly was entailed. The house itself could not be sold. No, she was just a dream, and would die, as dreams die always.

In '43 changes of plans sent me back to Cornwall, with my three children. I had not visited Menabilly since the war began. No bombs had come her way, yet she looked like a blitzed building. The shutters were not shuttered now. The panes were broken. She had been left to die.

It was easy to climb through the front windows. The house was stripped and bare. Dirty paper on the floor. Great fungus growths from the ceiling. Moisture everywhere, death and decay. I could scarcely see the soul of her for the despair. The mould was in her bones.

Odd, yet fearful, what a few years of total neglect can do to a house, as to a man, a woman . . . . Have you seen a man who has once been handsome and strong go unshaven and unkempt? Have you seen a woman lovely in her youth raddled beneath the eyes, her hair tousled and grey?

Sadder than either, more bitter and more poignant, is a lonely house.

I returned to my furnished cottage, in angry obstinate mood. Something was dying, without hope of being saved. And I would not stand it. Yet there was nothing I could do. Nothing? There was one faint, ridiculous chance in a million . . . . I telephoned my lawyer and asked him to write to the owner of Menabilly and ask him to let the house to me for a term of years. "He won't consent for a moment," I said. "It's just a shot at random."

But the shot went home . . . . A week later my lawyer came to see me.

"By the way," he said, "I believe you will be able to rent Menabilly. But you must treat it as a whim, you know. The place is in a fearful state. I doubt if you could do more than camp out there occasionally."

I stared at him in amazement. "You mean—he would consent?" I said.

"Why, yes, I gather so," answered my lawyer.

Then it began. Not the Battle of Britain, not the attack upon the soft underbelly of Europe that my husband was helping to conduct from Africa, but my own private war to live in Menabilly by the time winter came again . . . .

"You're mad . . . you're crazy . . . you can't do it . . . there's no lighting . . . there's no water . . . there's no heating . . . you'll get no servants . . . it's impossible!"

I stood in the dining room, surrounded by a little team of experts. There was the architect, the builder, the plumber, the electrician, and my lawyer, with a ruler in his hand which he waved like a magic baton.

"I don't think it can be done . . . ." And my answer always, "Please, please, see if it can be done."

The creeper cut from the windows. The windows mended. The men upon the roof mortaring the slates. The carpenter in the house, setting up the doors. The plumber in the well, measuring the water. The electrician on the ladder, wiring the walls. And the doors and windows open that had not been open for so long. The sun warming the cold dusty rooms. Fires of brushwood in the grates. And then the scrubbing of the floors that had felt neither brush nor mop for many years. Relays of charwomen, with buckets and swabs. The house alive with men and women. Where did they come from? How did it happen? The whole thing was an impossibility in wartime. Yet it did happen. And the gods were on my side. Summer turned to autumn, autumn to December. And in December came the vans of furniture; and the goods and chattels I had stored at the beginning of the war and thought never to see again were placed, like fairy things, about the rooms at Menabilly.

Like fairy things, I said, and looking back, after living here two years, it is just that. A fairy tale. Even now I have to pinch myself to know that it is true. I belong to the house. The house belongs to me.

From the end of the lawn where I first saw her, that May morning, I stand and look upon her face. The ivy is stripped. Smoke curls from the chimneys. The windows are flung wide. The doors are open. My children come running from the house on to the lawn. The hydrangeas bloom for me. Clumps of them stand on my piano.

Slowly, in a dream, I walk towards the house. "It's wrong," I think, "to love a block of stone like this, as one loves a person. It cannot last. It cannot endure. Perhaps it is the very insecurity of the love that makes the passion strong. Because she is not mine by right. The house is still entailed, and one day will belong to another . . . ."

I brush the thought aside. For this day, and for this night, she is mine.

And at midnight, when the children sleep, and all is

hushed and still, I sit down at the piano and look at the panelled walls, and slowly, softly, with no one there to see, the house whispers her secrets, and the secrets turn to stories, and in strange and eerie fashion we are one, the house and I.

MOVING HOUSE

[1969]

Moving house, after twenty-six years, is rather like facing
a major operation. Especially if the home one leaves behind has been greatly loved. As a young woman I moved
often, being married to a soldier, and we were never more
than eighteen months in the same place. This did not
greatly worry me, because my husband organised everything, even to writing out the labels for the removal men
and deciding where the various pieces of furniture should
go. He would always try to make the new home as much
like the old one as possible, for, although very go-ahead
and progressive as a soldier, he was a stickler for routine in
personal life. So, while desks were placed in new living
rooms in identical corners beside new fireplaces, and while
he arranged the familiar objects in the right order, I would
wander around in a daze, trying to picture the sort of
people who had lived in the house before. Also I felt sorry
for the house we had left; I was sure it would be melancholy without us. This feeling passed, and soon I would
"grow" into the new house, taking something of its atmosphere into myself and giving something in return. Anyway,
we were both young, and life was an adventure.

When the war came and my husband was serving over-
seas, I took a bold step and moved house on my own, with
a nanny and three young children. I rented the old manor
house Menabilly that I had written about in *Rebecca*,
which had no electricity and no hot-water system, and was

full of dry rot. My husband, in far-off Tunis, told his brother officers, "I am afraid Daphne has gone mad."

The madness paid off. When he came on leave for Christmas, expecting to find us squatting in camp beds with the rain pouring through the roof, he found the telephone installed, electric light in all the rooms, a hot bath waiting, and the furniture brought from store and put in just the right places he would have chosen himself. There were sprays of holly behind every picture.

"Well, I must confess, I didn't know you had it in you," he told me.

He grew to love it as much as I did, and forever after, during his lifetime, Christmas was always the high spot of the year.

In 1964 we knew that our lease was coming to an end and that we should have to look for another home. The thought of moving from this particular bit of Cornwall was unbearable to both of us, and, like a miracle, unspoken prayer was answered. The lease of the one-time dower house to Menabilly, Kilmarth, fell vacant, and it was only half a mile or so away, with a splendid view over the sea beloved so well. We walked round the empty rooms, as desolate as Menabilly had been before we lived there, and he said to me, "I like this place. I can see ourselves here." He signed the lease a few weeks before he died.

This was all of four years ago, and in the intervening period, between writing books, I have been planning what I hope will be my final home. I moved into Kilmarth in June of this year, 1969, and count myself very fortunate that I had so much time to make the change. Day by day, week by week, month by month, I would visit the empty house, walk round the rooms, plan the decorations, watch the necessary alterations, decide where the furniture would ultimately go. The architect, the builder, the builder's craftsmen, could not have been more helpful or more kind. We felt ourselves a team, creating a renewed Kilmarth which I felt very certain its predecessors had loved.

The Roger Kylmerth who lived here in 1327 may have been different in character from the one I have written about in my novel *The House on the Strand*, but the foundations of his home are beneath me now. The Bakers, merchants in the seventeenth century, touched these walls. Younger sons of Rashleigh parents bided here before inheriting Menabilly, rebuilding upwards from the foundations, while later tenants, so I am told, kept packs of collie dogs and even peacocks! I like to think of the latter strutting the walk where I now exercise my own West Highland terriers.

Kilmarth, today, has a slated eighteenth-century front, with twentieth-century additions on either side. The front garden is enclosed by walls and railings, giving a formal touch, and, although it was suggested I should take down the Victorian porch, I am glad I kept it; it has a delightful, old-fashioned air. The drawing room, or long room as I call it, is on the right of the hall, and to the left are my small dining room and library. When the doors of all three are opened you can see from one end of the house to the other, thus giving a sense of space. The french windows of the long room have been opened wide all summer long, facing due south, and I can see myself sitting here through the winter too.

The original dining room of my predecessors, three steps up from the hall, has been turned into a kitchen. Light paper on the walls, a warm brick-coloured floor and modern wall units with an electric cooker, this is one of the nicest rooms in the house. Once it was dark and narrow, but a wide window now gives light where the chimney breast used to be. The cramped rooms beyond, used in old days for staff or nursery, are now a separate suite for visit-

131

ing grandchildren. The little ones can romp, the teen-agers play their pop records, and their grandmother in the front of the house be none the wiser! What is more, they have their own staircase and their own entry, and the wing has all the appearance of a miniature house on its own.

The basement, useful for storage now, held the one time kitchen, pantries, laundry, stillroom of former tenants, no longer practicable today. Here are the cellar walls of antiquity, and I have turned one recess into a tiny chapel. To exorcise unquiet spirits? Perhaps. Who knows, it may have been a place for prayer in centuries past. The yard without, which surely once led from the mediaeval farmhouse building, has been relaid with the cobbled stones that, now lying about the grounds, may have graced it long ago.

Let us make our way above once more to the front of the house. The staircase leads to my own quarters, and to the guest rooms for family and friends. Here I admit to doing myself in style. Furnishings and fabrics are not new, they have been with me for much of my married life, but I have never before had a suite of dressing room, bathroom and bedroom; and the view from the bedroom, which over-looks the sea, is the best I have ever known. Ships anchor in the bay before proceeding to Par Harbour, and the ilex trees have a magic quality, outlined against the sky. It is a very pleasant room by day or night. The guest room along the landing I call the pink room. It contains my father's four-poster bed, and the closet adjoining is now a bath-room. A narrow corridor leads to two double guest rooms and one single room, with their own bathroom and W.C. So when Christmas comes again I can, at a pinch, put up children, grandchildren, in fact the entire family, although there might be a certain amount of juggling with camp beds.

I hope, in time, to get the overgrown garden back into

some sort of order. Last spring I planted dahlias, but none of them came up. The roses had the blight. Most of the undergrowth and brambles have been cleared, and new grass sown where the nettles grew. The apple trees are long past their prime, but the windfalls have gone into apple tart on Sundays. My husband's old boat stands in her final resting place, and she shall have a coat of paint next spring. And so I look about me, planning the months ahead: one day, perhaps, reclaim the tennis court in the orchard, where Victorian ladies played patball with one another, though for tennis I feel it has probably had its day. A football pitch might be the answer for growing grandsons. Two meadows lie beyond, let for grazing to the neighbouring farmer, and I shall have to watch any battles between Chelsea and Spurs in case the flying ball should fall amongst, and startle, his pedigree herd of cattle.

I shall miss the acres of woodland that surround Menabilly. Here the only "plantations" worthy of the name are those bordering the road leading to the village of Polkerris, and a winding shrubbery at the back of the house. Never mind. Wildlife abounds here as much as there. Badgers scratch the earth beneath tumbled leaves, jackdaws roost in the taller trees, owls hoot by night, and the long summer through swallows and martins built under the eaves. As for butterflies, the place abounds with them. Tortoiseshell, swallowtail, admirals, flit amongst the overgrown buddleia, and so, I regret to say, do wasps as well.

The pleasantest spot at evening is an old summerhouse, built by one of my predecessors, where one can sit sheltered from cold winds and watch the sun go down across the bay. Steps lead down from the wall to the field below. Perhaps a peacock strutted here, his tail spread wide. And the collies surely rampaged in search of erring sheep. For my own part, rejoicing in a long hot summer, I have crossed the field most afternoons after tea and descended to the cliffs and the beach beyond. The sea, milky white from the sediment of china clay, has a strange attraction, to me at any rate, though I have heard grumbles at its stickiness from summer visitors. At high spring tides the water laps the cliffs and there is a strong undertow, dangerous, I would think, to the non-swimmer. Now, with the visitors departed, the only intruders upon the beach are oyster catchers and gulls.

Indeed, I tell myself, as I climb the steep hill back again to Kilmarth (Thrombosis Hill, I have called it, and time will prove if it lives up to its name), I am most blest and truly fortunate. The house I looked upon with misgivings before I moved, wondering whether I should ever settle down in new surroundings, no longer gives me the somewhat dubious impression of a pleasant holiday residence lent to me for a season by obliging friends, but is transforming itself, day by day, week by week, with the familiar furniture and objects all about me, into the friendly warmth and comfort of a place well loved, where I am made welcome. In short, we are at one, and I am at home.

A WINTER'S AFTERNOON, KILMARTH

It is the idle half-hour succeeding lunch, when, having
written a number of unnecessary letters all morning, I can
sip black coffee and smoke the first cigarette of the day.
The back pages of yesterday's newspapers are still unread,
and it is my whim to contrast the current weather report
with the advertisements for winter holidays in Cornwall.

"The ridge of low pressure now approaching our
western sea-board will deepen, and the showers at present
falling on the Scilly Isles and Cornwall will become heavy
at times, turning to hail and thunder on higher ground.
Winds will increase to gale force, veering southwesterly to
west, and later in the day temperatures may fall to 28
degrees. Outlook for the next two days cold and unsettled,
with gales locally."

I glance out of the window. My informant on the radio
was right. The pine trees beyond the garden wall, planted
by some Victorian predecessor in the belief that whatever
suited the Scottish climate would defy the elements equally
well in Cornwall—and how wise he was—are beginning to
sway, while massive clouds, driven by some demon force,
bank the far horizon, reminding me of a rather too
elaborate production of *Macbeth*.

I turn to the advertisements in the newspapers. "Double
Your Sunshine and Come to Lovely Looe." Looe is a few
miles along the coast, and that foremost cloud, vast as a
witch's trailing cloak, will be upon it in exactly four
minutes. There are, however, further blandishments west-
ward across the bay. "Visit Mevagissey, the Fishing Village

135

with the Continental Touch." Mevagissey is already blotted out with rain, but doubtless some winter visitor, lured by summer memories of the Côte d'Azur, is now scurrying from the quayside in search of a casino with an affable croupier in charge bidding him *"Faites vos jeux."* There may be one or two slot machines still in action, but I doubt it.

The hotels along the coast offer more tempting vistas still. "A gleaming jewel on a sun-drenched bay. Balconies to every bedroom . . ." But enough. Being myself no visitor to these shores, but an inhabitant, on and off, for over forty years, and having recently moved from a sheltered house in woodlands to my present home on "higher ground" threatened by that same hail and thunder announced over the radio, I am anxious to prove my mettle. There is, perhaps, an "Award Scheme for Courage Displayed by the Over-Sixties" brewing in the minds of princes, and I could qualify. Besides, the dog needs exercise.

Dressed like Tolstoy in his declining years, fur cap with ear flaps, padded jerkin and rubber boots to the knee, I venture forth. Moray, my West Highland terrier, taking one look at the sky, backs swiftly into the porch, but brutally I urge him on, and we cross the garden to the fields beyond. Where I lived before, at Menabilly, there was a shaded path known as the Palm Walk, and on rainy or windy days, flanked by tall trees, I could amble along it peacefully, snipping at the drooping heads of blue hydrangeas still in bloom. Here, at Kilmarth, I know no such lassitude. The sloping field I am bound to traverse, if I walk at all, is under plough, and the herd of South Devon cattle who tramp daily across the as yet unsown soil, having first satiated themselves with roots a little further down, have turned the field into another Passchendaele. "This," I tell myself, "is what Tommy endured as a subaltern in the First

World War," and, inspired by the thought, I sink into craters made by the South Devons, wondering if Mr. Mitchell the farmer could have crossbred his prize herd with yaks from Tibet. The cattle, less courageous than myself, did not linger long on the "higher ground" but have already sought shelter in the farmyard out of sight, having advanced milking time by at least two hours.

Shaking my feet clear of Passchendaele, and avoiding the electric fence that guards the roots, I climb over the stile that leads to the grazing land above the cliffs, thinking how closely I must resemble a veteran at the Battle of Ypres. Moray, flicking his ears, runs like a greyhound to a favourite molehill, which he is wont to anoint as a matter of routine. This ritual, if nothing else, will make his day. Mr. Mitchell's flock of sheep, taking him for a marauder and mistaking the action, begin to scatter. Heavy with lamb, some of them strangely decorated about the head with brambles, they have the bizarre crowned appearance of beasts bound for some sacrificial slaughter. Remembering the doomed flock plunging over the cliffs to destruction in the film of *Far from the Madding Crowd*, I hold my breath; but after a brief and hesitating pause they labour up the hill in a northwesterly direction, making for home, and I breathe again. It is Moray and I who turn seaward to brave the full force of the gale.

It is a stupendous sight that meets my eyes. Thirteen ships are anchored in the bay, rolling their guts out in a cauldron sea. I can make out a couple of Dutchmen, a Dane, a German, and I think a Norwegian flag amongst them, but the shelter of Par Harbour will not be theirs this night, for it is already high water, and the docks are full. What if their cables drag, a mile distant, off this lee shore? The only hope up-steam and out of it, rounding the Gribben head to the Fowey estuary.

I put up my arm in salutation, not to the courage of the

seamen on board but in a vain attempt to keep the hail out of my eyes. Below me the sea thunders on Bûly beach, so called because of the white stones—*bûly*—that lie upon it. Rounded, flat, scattered here and there upon the sand, these stones make excellent targets on a summer's day for the anointing Moray while I swim. Now, as the incoming rollers break upon them and lash the cliffs, only to withdraw with an ominous sucking sound, the white stones have a ghastly resemblance to drowning ewes, and for a moment I fear that my vision of the scene from *Far from the Madding Crowd* has in part come true. The stones do not loll, though, in the surf but remain submerged, and I am spared winning an award for gallantry and plunging to the rescue of mangled carcasses; indeed I could not have done so, for the descent to the beach itself is swept by a sea at least six feet high. This is disappointing. There is a cave on Bûly beach into which the hail would not have penetrated, and, although it is damp and eerie and smells of old bones, had it been half tide I could have stood there like Prospero, watching the storm, the faithful Moray Ariel at my side.

Which reminds me, where *is* Moray? I look about me, shouting in vain against the wind. Seized with sudden panic, I climb up the stony track, away from the beach, to the cliffs above. I can just see his white rump disappearing along the muddied path in the direction of the only shelter known to his dog instinct, a hedge of thorn about a hundred yards distant that overhangs a drop known locally as Little Hell. The place is aptly named. God knows what drowning seafarer in centuries past caught a glimpse of it from an upturned boat and cursed it as he sank. Or, perchance, an irate farmer, predecessor of Mr. Mitchell from Trill Farm, driven to frenzy by a scolding wife, hurled himself and her to merciful oblivion. Either, or all three, dubbed the spot thus. The ravine is cut out of the cliff face, and the potential suicide is only spared from the goal he seeks by a strand of barbed wire, and what appears to be the single bar of an old bedstead—doubtless forming part of the frenzied farmer's connubial couch—with three straggling thronbushes beyond. He cannot see the depths below, so steep is the incline, and a torn sack masks the final sickening drop, but at high tide, as it is today, an evil hiss surges some two hundred feet beneath him, fair warning of the fate awaiting trespass.

Moray has sense, all the same. The thornbushes, bent backwards over the muddied path, make an effective arbour in a space about three feet square; it is, in fact, our only haven in a world gone temporarily mad. He awaits me, hunched and disapproving.

We crouch side by side above Little Hell, enduring some of that same discomfort which political prisoners experienced in the torture chamber of the Tower of London known as Little Ease, but at least the hail is no longer in my face and the rain is driving slantways above my head, missing my humped knees by a few inches. It is some comfort to think of all the things I would rather *not* be doing. Ringing the front doorbell of people I don't know well, but whose invitation to drinks has been reluctantly accepted, and as the door opens being met by the conversational roar of those guests already arrived . . . Standing in the model gown department of a smart London store, endeavouring to squeeze myself into an outfit designed for someone half my age, and, as I grapple with a zip fastener that will not meet, becoming aware of the bored and pitying eye of the saleswoman in charge . . . Circling any airport in a fog, or worse still, waiting for the fog to lift and sitting in the airport lounge hemmed in by bores, all them bent on exchanging their life history . . .

Meditation, after twenty minutes or so, is cut short by the realisation that a stream from the field above, which disappeared mysteriously under the muddied path on

which I crouch, is pouring its tumbling waters into a miniature Niagara behind my back, before descending to Little
Hell. It is time to move. Struggling to my feet and glancing
upward, I perceive that, miraculously, the hail has ceased,
the black pall of the sky has parted into jagged shades of
blue, and the sun itself it breaking through, gold, all-
powerful, like the face of God. The scene is utterly transformed. The rollers in the bay are milky white, boisterous,
lovely, even wilder than before, and graced now with the
sun's touch, all malevolence gone. The vessels plunging at
their cables dance as if to a fairground's tune, and one of
them, the Dutchman, lets forth a siren blast of triumph and
begins to move slowly, majestically, towards Par Harbour.
   The port is jammed with shipping. Every berth seems
full. Derricks appear to intertwine, crisscrossed at every
angle, and now that the wind has shifted a few points west
it brings the welcome sound of industry, power plants at
work, engines whining, men hammering, chimneys pouring out great plumes of smoke, white and curling like the
sea. Pollution? Nonsense, the sight is glorious! Later the
remaining ships at anchor will dock in turn, load up with
china clay, and plough back across the Channel to their
home-port destination. The white waste from the clay, re-
gretted by some, scatters a filmy dust upon the working
sheds, and the bay itself has all the froth and dazzle of a
milk churn spilt into a turbulent pool. Tourists may seek
the golden sands of holiday brochures if they like, but to
swim in such a sea is ecstasy—I have tried it, and I know!
   Suddenly, out of nowhere, the birds appear. Oyster
catchers, with their panic call and rapid wingbeat; curlews,
more mysterious, aloof, the whistling cry surely portending
sorrow, and then like leaves uptossed in all directions, but
swerving, dipping, to their leader's flight; a flock of star-
lings, soaring for the sheer joy of motion, their ultimate
destination the ploughed fields of Passchendaele above.

Which, cowardlike, I cannot face. Not for a second time this afternoon those craters and muddied depths. Nor the climb itself, so easy to descend, but seen from Little Hell the peak of Everest itself. So, for Moray and myself, the easier gradient of the cliff path that will finally lead us in roundabout fashion to a little wood of about four and a half acres, which forms part of Kilmarth domain.

My lease made mention of certain "sporting rights," and for this splendid bonus I pay a shilling a year. I am not sure what I had in mind when the lease was signed. Possibly sons-in-law wearing tweeds, armed with Purdey guns and calling "Over" as pheasants swerved above their heads, the same pheasants gracing the dinner table at a later date. Or, on a less ambitious note, the more doubtful pleasure of lunching on pigeon pie (I read once that pigeon eaten on three consecutive days brought certain death). Be that as it may, the pheasant's call and the pigeon's flutter are alike absent this afternoon; the only thing to stir except the trees themselves is a ragged crow, who launches himself from a dead branch at my approach and croaks his way to Passchendaele.

It is not everyone, however, who is sole tenant of sporting rights, and, as Moray plunges into the wood and I pitch after him, I must admit I walk the narrow path with a certain swagger. Possession is short-lived. As I trip over a rhododendron root and round a corner, I come upon an elderly man leaning against a tree, a gun at the ready. Moray barks, and he turns and stares. Is this the moment to stand, as they say, my ground? One of my predecessors at Kilmarth, a formidable lady by all accounts, who held sway some fifty years ago and was said to commune with the spirit world, had for escort when she walked a flock of peacocks, a pack of collie dogs and a donkey wearing a beribboned hat; she would have handled the situation with aplomb. Not so her present-day successor.

I advance timidly, forming appropriate words of welcome. "Any luck?"

He shakes his head. I shrug in sympathy. "Too bad, it must be the weather. Well, don't shoot yourself instead of the absent birds."

I wave a cheerful hand as I pass, and the slow smile that spreads across his features suggests that the impression I have made is poor. Ah, well . . . He must have walked and shot that wood, man and boy, for nearly fifty years. I am the intruder, not he, and as I shuffle along beneath the dripping trees I no longer swagger. Moray, of course, is disgusted with me. The ankles of all strange men are suspect, and the elderly sportsman promised easy game. He follows me, muttering, and I "shush" him under my breath, relieved when the wood is left behind and I climb through the fence to the plot of garden surrounding the house itself. Here, at least, I am mistress of all I survey, and I can relieve my sporting inclinations by fetching a long pruning implement, during the ten minutes of fine weather that remains, and beheading the grotesque tops of a clump of bamboos which, shaking in the wind and masking the sea view from one of the windows, have the horrible appearance of African witch doctors engaged in some tribal rite. I attack them with ferocity, and then, arms aching, honour satisfied, make my way indoors before the hail strikes. The thought of tea is doubly welcome after these efforts, legs stretched out before flaming logs.

I fling off my Tolstoy outfit, replace the pruning implement, and open the door of my living room.

I am driven back by clouds of evil-smelling smoke. The pile of logs, balanced with such loving care before I set out for the walk, the paper beneath them gently touched with a lighted match, instead of welcoming me with the roaring blaze I had expected has turned jet black. Not even a tongue of flame arises from them. I kneel beside the grate, bellows in hand, but not so much as a spark glints from the stinking ashes. I sit back on my heels in despair, remembering all the remaining logs awaiting transport from the old boiler room in the basement. These were to see me through the winter, and I have no others. Hewn from a giant fir laid low in the autumn by a crosscut saw, they were my pride and joy as much as the sporting rights.

I hurry to the nether regions to bring up kindling wood, but this has been cut from the same fir, and when laid upon the corpses of the blackened logs it emits one protesting spark, sighs and is extinguished. Too late to double back to the wood and search for twigs of stouter brand. I should lose yet more face before the sportsman with the gun, and anyway the heavens have burst again; what momentary glory shone from the sky has gone forever.

> Pear logs and apple logs
> They will scent your room.
> Cherry logs across the dogs
> Smell like flowers in bloom.

Somewhere, in a desk, I have the whole poem about logs, sent to me by an obliging friend and expert, recommending those that give warmth and scent, and warning against those that do not. Feverishly I search for it amongst a heap of papers, and run my eye down the printed page.

> Fir logs it is a crime
> For anyone to sell.

I never thought to read the poem before having the fir tree felled....

> Holly logs will burn like wax,
> You should burn them green.

I can bear no more of it, and go to the kitchen to make tea, but as I drink it in front of the non-existent fire, wearing dark glasses to protect my eyes from the festoons of smoke hanging like Christmas decorations about the panelled room, I think of the many stunted hollies in the shrubbery behind the house, and plan destruction.

Tea passes without further incident, and supper on a tray watching television—a play showing teen-agers making love on one channel and a very old film about the American navy in Korea on the other, offering doubtful entertainment to my jaded palate—takes me up to bedtime.

The increasing sound of the gale without and lashing rain against the windows gives warning that there is one remaining hazard to face before I climb the stairs. Moray must be put out, not at the front door where he would be blown over the wall and never seen again, but down to those same nether regions where the logs are harboured, and through the hatch door of the boiler room opening on the "patio," where he can do his worst in comparative shelter.

The winding stair to the basement does not deter me, nor the memory of those characters dead for centuries who may have walked the basement in days gone by. Fourteenth-century yeomen, sixteenth-century merchants, eighteenth- and nineteenth-century parsons and squires, are shades that I can brave with equanimity. The idea of the Edwardian lady, however, who communed with the spirit world flanked by her peacocks, is more disturbing. It was in the basement kitchen no longer used as such that she used to give her orders for the day to the trembling cook, and I have it on good authority that a parrot, chained to its perch, let fly a torrent of abuse at her approach. I stand shivering at the hatch door, while Moray sniffs the cobbles in disdain, and then, to test both our nerves, I switch out the light. This surely should bring an award for stamina.

Nothing happens. No clatter of a cane upon stone flags.

No screech from protesting peacocks. No cry of "Pieces of eight . . . pieces of eight . . ." from the parrot. A door bangs in the distance, but this is probably the draught. My formidable predecessor of more affluent days may be a silent witness to my challenge, but thank heaven she does not materialise. May she rest in peace.

The door is bolted, Moray scampers ahead of me up the winding stair, and we proceed to our own quarters and the bedroom that was, I am glad to say, built on in later years, after the peacock lady's day. It faces seaward, and thus receives the full force of the sou'westerly, or indeed of any gale, but the effect of this is stimulating, like being on the enclosed bridge of a ship, without the rocking. I look out of the window and see the riding lights of those vessels that have not yet sought refuge in Par Harbour, and the thought of the seamen possibly battened down below, at the mercy of every lurching sea, makes me turn to my own bed with a sense of well-being, even of complacency. Moray retires to his lair and, leaning back on my pillows with a sigh of satisfaction, I open the unfinished newspaper I was reading after lunch. "You too can enjoy the thrills of camping in Cornwall." Brushing the advertisement impatiently aside, I turn to matters of greater moment. The thrust and parry of political parties, the feuds and international problems of our time.

Something splashes upon my pillow. An ominous drip. It is followed in a moment by a second, and then a third. A tear from an unseen presence? I look up to the ceiling and perceive, all complacency gone, that a row of beads, like a very large rosary swinging from a nun's breast, is forming a chain immediately above my head and fast turning into bubbles. Drip . . . drip . . . The water torture, practised in the Far East and said to be more swiftly effective than our own mediaeval rack. Hypnotised, I watch the row of beads expand and fall, its place immediately taken by another, meanwhile my pillow taking on the sodden appearance of the sack cast away at Little Hell.

This is the end . . . . I will *not* be forced out of the double bed I have slept in for thirty-five years and seek asylum elsewhere. No heating switched on in the spare rooms, beds not aired, lamps lacking bulbs.

"You too can enjoy the thrill of camping in Cornwall."

I leap out on to the floor and, risking hernia, proceed to drag my double bed into the centre of the room. The floorboards groan. Moray, disturbed from sound sleep, sits up and stares at me, a look of intense astonishment on his face. "What on *earth* . . . ?"

I fetch towels for the cascade to splash upon, and then, marooned on a flat surface, headboard gone, pillowless, install myself on the desert island that has become my bed. Moray continues to look astonished, even aggrieved.

Tommy's photograph, beret at the familiar jaunty angle, smiles at me from the dry wall opposite. I am reminded, only too well, that it was always my berth, in our old sailing days, never his, which suffered the inevitable leaks from the deck above. My discomfort produced delighted chuckles, and although the following day the leaks would be stopped, with each successive craft we owned the one wet patch would invariably form itself, in an otherwise perfect boat, over my head.

The smile is infectious, and whether a happy echo from an unforgettable past, or a signal from the Isles of the Blest, it has the required result. Sense of humour returns. I make a long arm and switch off the light, reckoning up the follies of one more useless day, yet knowing in my heart that, but for the absence of the departed skipper, I would not change it for the world.

SUNDAY

[1976]

"Six days shalt thou labour, and do all that thou hast to do; but the seventh day is the sabbath of the Lord thy God. On it thou shalt do no manner of work . . . ."

Yes, but even in the time of Moses animals had to be cared for and fed, the lost sheep sought and brought back to the fold, fires kindled in winter, water brought from the well. Farmers do the same today. Railwaymen drive trains for those who must travel. Seamen man ships. Pilots guide aeroplanes. These people labour, though many others take their ease. The Jewish Sabbath—still sacrosanct, I understand—became the model, through the centuries, of the Christian Sunday, when almost everybody, men, women, children, went to church to do homage to their Maker.

The numbers have decreased in the mid-twentieth century, and the faithful are mostly middle-aged. Why so? Churchmen, laymen, scholars, attenders and non-attenders argue the reasons, the more frequent excuse being that there is more to do for a family on Sunday nowadays than ever there was in the past. Outings, picnics, family gatherings, television, or simply rising late and reading the Sunday papers. The habit has been lost. Church bells are no longer a summons. Religious conscience is stilled. Belief in the Maker is dormant, if it exists at all.

As a writer, a widow, approaching seventy years of age, how do I look upon Sunday? Possibly the answer to this goes back into childhood.

147

At five or six Sunday meant putting on clean under-clothes, which were prickly and uncomfortable. Woollen combinations and stockings that itched. A different dress from weekdays. And because it was my actor father Gerald's day of rest, we children were bidden downstairs to shake hands with his friends before they departed for golf. This was shy-making, a penance. Then, at a slightly older age, came Going to Church. Matins was dull. But my aunt, who was also my godmother, was a fervent High Anglican, and when I accompanied her to high mass I thoroughly enjoyed it; there was plenty to watch, like go-ing to the theatre. One thing worried me, however, whether at matins or at mass, and this was the humble, even obsequious attitude of all the adults to their Maker. "We are miserable sinners . . . there is no health in us." Why must they cringe and crawl? Surely this was not what God wanted? So later, when my father Gerald, who never went to church, suggested that I should go for a walk with him on Hampstead Heath instead, I readily agreed. His religion consisted of being kind and generous to people "down on their luck," and of kissing the photographs of all his dead family, father, mother, brother and sisters, be-fore he went to bed. I saw the point of this. It made sense, perhaps, to God too.

Nowadays, with one sister a High Anglican like my god-mother and the other a Roman Catholic, I still do not attend either matins or mass. But, because I have a deep respect for Christianity, I read a Catholic missal every Sun-day morning after breakfast. A slight show-off, in a way, because I like to test my Latin. And this particular missal was published by Monseigneur Gaspard Lefebvre, who of late has been in trouble with the Pope.

And after reading the Mass for the Day, what then? I do my weekly accounts and pay all outstanding bills, which at least puts me right with any debts. Then, as my housekeeper has the day to herself, I cook my lunch, so testing my culinary talent. Sometimes a great success. Sometimes a slight failure. But no matter whichever way it goes. And observing the old Sabbath rule, I never "work" on Sundays. By working I mean writing, which has been my profession for forty-five years. But I do clear up my mail and answer outstanding letters. Then a walk, or in summer a swim, and afterwards long hours with the Sunday papers. Starting, naturally enough, with the *Sunday Telegraph.*

It is a day which, unless members of my family happen to be staying with me, I invariably keep to myself. I give no invitations and accept none. A day for privacy, except for neighbouring cattle and sheep, with which I am on excellent terms, speaking to them in their own language. (I baa better than I moo, nevertheless they appear to understand the drift of my conversation; even Romany of Trill, the bull, acknowledges my presence with a courteous inclination of his horns.) As to the birds, they flock to the bird table in winter for their food, ignoring my welcoming twitter. I can hear them chattering amongst themselves: "Silly old fool, eat up and don't take any notice of her, she's quite harmless," upon which I tactfully withdraw, and observe them from the cover of a window.

It may be thought, by churchgoing readers, that during the course of this peaceful Sunday I continue to neglect my Maker. On the contrary, conversing with beast and bird is my way of giving thanks. And if anything deepens belief in a Creator, it is by watching wildlife in the countryside, a constant miracle, and noting the changes in their routine through the four seasons; something that applies equally to the colour and growth of trees, plants and shrubs, even weeds. They all obey natural law, which is surely God's law.

One of the greatest miracles of all is the migration of swallows. The first week in May I stand in my small front

149

garden and wait and watch. They never fail to arrive, though not always on a Sunday. I wave "Hurrah, and welcome!" and they make for my roof, or the old nest inside my garage that was their home the preceding year. Here they rear their young, generally two broods, and by September they begin to prepare for the autumn flight. They fly overhead in a restless manner. "Safe journey, and a good winter!" I call. The following day they have gone. They are obeying natural law.

There are several questions I would like to ask the Creator, though—and this is one fault I find in my missal, that nobody asks a question—and one of the questions is, "In prehistoric days, before You thought of man, were You evolving too, and occasionally making mistakes? If not, why create species like the brontosaurus, like the mammoth, like other gigantic beasts, and let the species die, unless at the period of their creation and development You had a thing about size, and thought big was best? Then gradually realised You had made an error of judgement. Yes or no?"

A simple question, but a direct answer would be helpful. If an error is admitted, then there must have been others through the ages. Faulty genes, chromosomes, in man, which cannot be blamed on man himself. And what about the million million stars? Have some of them life? Must they be swallowed up eventually, and our world too, by something called a black hole? Someone will say that it is not for us to question the mind of the Creator. I disagree. Curiosity is a fundamental instinct within all of us. So these are some of the things I ponder about upon a Sunday afternoon, sitting, perhaps, at what I call the Look-Out, staring down across the fields to the sea. Then I come indoors and make myself a cup of tea, the hall sadly empty since the death of my faithful dog companion in the summer heat wave, my constant shadow for twelve years. I will replace him in the spring with a couple of pups, and life, along with natural law, will continue.

Telephone calls to my family follow. Everybody well and happy? Good. I can settle with an easy mind to television for the rest of the evening, switching channels at whim; the faster the police chase in New York or San Francisco the more relaxed I am, sloping into my chair, only to sit up with a jerk and realise I have missed the dénouement. Time for bed, for filling hot-water bottles, for saying my prayers. Sunday is over.

"Give peace in our time, O Lord. And may those who by Thy counsel lead the peoples of this earth give a right judgement."

POEMS

THE WRITER

[1926]

Not for me the arrow in the air,
    Nor the mountain snows,
    Nor the dumb ocean,
    Nor the wind on the heath,
    Nor the warm breath
Of the bare bright sun upon my hair.

Not for me the mist of the white stars,
    Nor the singing falls
    Nor the deep river,
    Nor the flung foam
    Upon the hard beach,
Nor the other mountains that I cannot reach.

Mine is the silence
And the quiet gloom
Of a clock ticking
In an empty room,
The scratch of a pen,
Ink-pot and paper,
And the patter of the rain.
Nothing but this as long as I am able,
Firelight—and a chair, and a table.

Not for me the whisper in the ear,
   Nor the touch of a hand,
   And that hand on my heart,
   Nor the quick pattering of feet
   Upon the stair, nor laughter in the street,
   Nor the swift glance, intangible and dear.

Not for me the hunger in the night,
   And the strength of the lover
   Tired of his loving,
   Seeking after passion the broken rest,
   Bearing his body's weight upon my breast.

Mine is the silence
Of the still day,
When the shouting on the hills
Sounds far away,
The song of the thrush,
In the quiet woods,
And the scent of trees.

Always the child who loved too late,
The poet—the fool—the watchman at the gate.
I am the actress mother who must make
A pretended cradle of her arms, lifeless and bare,
Who has never borne a child.
I am the deaf musician, calm and mild,
Singing a battle symphony, who has never heard the guns,
Nor the thunder in the air.

I am the painter whose blind gaze defiled
Would conjure an ocean, who has never seen the sea break
On the wild shores of Finistère . . .

Not for me the shadow of a smile,
   Nor the life that has gone,
   Nor the love that has fled,
   But the thread of the spider who spins on the wall,
   Who is lost, who is dead, who is nothing at all.

ANOTHER WORLD

[1947]

Last night the other world came much too near,
    And with it fear.
I heard their voices whisper me from sleep,
    And could not keep
My mind upon the dream, for still they came,
    Calling my name,
The loathly keepers of the netherland
    I understand.
My frozen brain rejects the pulsing beat;
    My willing feet,
Cloven like theirs, too swiftly recognise
    Without surprise.
The horn that echoes from the further hill,
    Discordant, shrill,
Has such a leaping urgency of song,
    Too loud, too long,
That prayer is stifled like a single note
    In the parched throat.
How fierce the flame! How beautiful and bright
    The inner light
Of that great world which lives within our own,
    Remote, alone.
Let me not see too soon, let me not know,
    And so forgo
All that I cling to here, the safety side
    Where I would bide.

Old Evil, loose my chains and let me rest
    Where I am best,
Here in the muted shade of my own dust.
    But if I must
Go wandering in Time and seek the source
    Of my life force,
Lend me your sable wings, that as I fall
    Beyond recall,
The sober stars may tumble in my wake,
    For Jesus' sake.

A PRAYER?

[1967]

Gentle Jesus, meek and mild,
Look upon a little child.

His the agony, the loss,
His the burden of your cross.
Mocked and scourged, with garments torn,
He must wear your crown of thorn.
Look upon his vale of tears
Flooded for two thousand years.
Hatred, bitterness and strife
Promise him eternal life.
In the tomb where you were lain,
Jewish boy and Arab slain
Kick the earth and bite the dust,
Victims of the law of lust.
Water once was changed to wine
In your name in Palestine,
Wine to blood flows merrily
On the shores of Galilee.
Falsely listened he who heard
Heaven's kingdom in your word.
This your message, blessed Lord,
Peace I bring not, but a sword.

Gentle Jesus, meek and mild,
Look upon a little child.